The Danvers Savings Bank, sponsor of
As the Century Turned, *was founded in 1850 to*
encourage thrift in local wage-earners and later to
assist them in building their homes.
By 1899, the bank was being hailed as "an
important factor in connection with the material
prosperity and growth of the town."
Today, at the turn of a new century, the Danvers
Savings Bank, steadfast in its determination to provide
a diversity of banking and investment services, has
expanded its offerings while remaining the area's only
independent, mutually-owned community bank.

Danvers SavingsBank
ONE CONANT ST.   DANVERS, MA 01923   508-777-2200

Girl Reading, circa 1894 by E. W. Merrill.

AS THE CENTURY TURNED
Photographic Glimpses of Danvers, Massachusetts

1880~1910

Richard P. Zollo
Richard B. Trask
and Joan M. Reedy

1989
A Centennial Publication
of the
Danvers Historical Society
Danvers, Massachusetts 01923

THE
DONNING COMPANY
PUBLISHERS
NORFOLK/VIRGINIA BEACH

"He must be an unreasonable creature, who having America for a continent, Massachusetts for a state, Essex for a county, and Danvers for a town, is not entirely satisfied."

Dr. Charles Sutherland Tapley, to whose memory we gratefully and affectionately dedicate this volume.

Charles S. Tapley, 1899, by C. S. Neal

The Donning Company/Publishers
5659 Virginia Beach Boulevard
Norfolk, Virginia 23502

Edited by Patricia Trainor-LeRoi
Richard A. Horwege, Senior Editor
Designed by Patrick Smith

Dust Jacket: Company K Marches down Elm Street and off to War, 1898.
Cover Logo: Lynne Clarkin
Front Endpapers: Danvers Square, circa 1893, by A. O. Elwell.
Title Page: Girl Reading, circa 1894, by E. W. Merrill.
Back Endpapers: 10 Berry Street, circa 1897, by E. W. Merrill.

Library of Congress Cataloging-in-Publication Data:

Zollo, Richard P., 1926-
As the century turned: photographic glimpses of Danvers, Massachusetts, 1880-1910/by Richard P. Zollo, Richard B. Trask, and Joan M. Reedy.
   p.   cm.
"A Centennial publication of the Danvers Historical Society."
Bibliography: p.
Includes index.
ISBN 0-89865-766-0

1. Danvers (Mass.)—Description—Views. 2. Danvers (Mass.)—Society life and customs—Pictorial works. I. Trask, Richard B., 1947- . II. Reedy, Joan M., 1960- . III. Title.
F74.D2Z65   1989   88-38216
974.4'5—dc 19   CIP

Printed in the United States of America

TABLE OF CONTENTS

Maple Street, Danvers, about 1890.

PREFACE

What was life like in Danvers between the years 1880 and 1910? A facile answer would be to echo Charles Dickens and say it was the best of times; it was the worst of times. In general, the times were good and promising to get better. This was true of many New England shoe towns. Without federal income taxes to pay, Francis Peabody lived like an English earl at The Lindens, and his relatives, the Endicotts, played decorously at farming around their Versailles, Glen Magna.

Those who labored long, hard hours over factory machines returned at night to homes or tenements that had more conveniences—running water and central heating, for example—than their parents had known. In season, a five-cent trolley ride took them to Salem Willows on Saturday nights or Sunday afternoons to enjoy the rides, dancing, and concerts.

The families of a growing number of merchants and manufacturers pursued culture with the tenacity of modern young people pumping exercise equipment. Poetry readings, piano recitals, and amateur theatricals from the stage of the Peabody Institute Library entertained and edified audiences. For those who traveled to Boston for the theater or the symphony, there was a late-night train back to Danvers.

What all these people were living through was a remarkable period of transition. Older citizens among them had grown up in a primarily agrarian culture with some manufacturing, a volunteer fire department, a small number of streets lit by gas, water from backyard wells, stagecoaches for public transportation, and a network of small, often inefficient railroad lines. The former abolitionists among these older citizens had turned their energies to eliminating intemperance and to gaining the vote for women. In an age that believed in building bridges, not burning them, old and young worked together in these two causes.

What life was becoming was summed up glowingly in an 1893 promotional publication, *Danvers—Representative Businessmen and Points of Interest*, which described the community as "a thoroughly live manufacturing town." By this time Danvers had, the booklet stated, an electric light department, concrete sidewalks, stores with "goods that sell at city prices," municipal fire and police departments, first-class street railways, and "a comprehensive railroad system."

What this description could also have included were an expanding water system, telephones, a huge new hospital for the treatment of the mentally ill, an improved public school system, two excellent preparatory schools, and a fine library. In 1901 the first locally owned automobile, a Stevens-Duryea, made its entrance into town.

What most distinguished this era in Danvers and nationally was a conviction that science, industrial growth, advancements in sanitation and medicine, and the inventiveness of engineers, like the town's Ralph O. Hood, were all working together to produce a better world for everyone, a world where children had an opportunity to enjoy a better standard of living than their parents had experienced.

Children played in a less restrictive environment. Born in 1883, Mabel Spofford recalled in 1958 hiking up the Putnamville train tracks as a little girl to the meadows near Burley Woods to pick bluets, dog-tooth violets, columbine, and hepaticas. On Sunday afternoon walks with her father and her brother Ralph, she engaged in a popular pastime, climbing Folly Hill to enjoy the view.

She also remembered one evening, after a sing-a-long in her grandparents' parlor, going down to the Eastern Division railroad station to welcome home the boys of Company K from the Spanish-American War. In recalling that incident, she later realized that life in the United States was becoming less innocent. Certainly several violent murders and robberies in this era marred what on the surface appeared to be a peaceful country town.

Perhaps it was the 1876 Centennial Exposition in Philadelphia that first made the country proud of its Anglo-American heritage and its growing industrial

Two of the buildings in which the Society kept rooms for meetings and the display of artifacts can be seen in this view of Danvers Square circa 1900. The earlier is the brick building on the right. It is the First National Bank, the successor to the old Village Bank. From 1897 until 1913, the Society occupied a suite of four rooms in the second, the Community Block, the hip-roofed Colonial Revival style building with the balustrade in the upper left. It was built in 1895 by Nathan T. Putnam for grocer James O. Perry, who employed ten assistants in his first-floor emporium. The most distinguished visitor to the Society's quarters was British Colonial Secretary Joseph Chamberlain, husband of Mary Endicott.

Here in one of the Society's rooms in the Community Block, a large portrait of Gen. Moses Porter hangs over the door. The general's career began at the Battle of Bunker Hill; his greatest feat was keeping the British fleet from landing troops at Norfolk, Virginia, during the War of 1812. The tri-color flag over the other door was taken during the Civil War from the British steamer Victory. The center picture above the display case between the two doors is of the first shoe factory in America, that of Zerubbabel Porter on Locust Street. The two Porters were brothers. An early project of society members was to contribute to their growing collections a teacup and saucer from their wedding china. Some of these are seen in the display case between the doors.

might. Locally, pride in their community's past led fifty-one citizens in 1889 to form the Danvers Historical Society. Inspired by their founder, Reverend Alfred Porter Putnam, who believed that the course of a nation's future could be determined by a study of the individuals and events of its past, members gave generously to the new organization. Among their gifts were their ancestors' letters, diaries, and account books, household items including textiles and furniture, military gear, relics, etc.

Before the century ended, this material was shown to the public in crowded display cases around a room in the First National Bank building on Maple Street. When a fire broke out there, these artifacts were rescued at some risk and moved farther up the Square to the Community Block, where the Society occupied a suite of four rooms.

To have a meeting house and museum of its own, the Society purchased the circa 1754 Page House in 1913, saving it from demolition, and moved it to its present site on Page Street. Here, in addition to its other activities like regular lecture series, trips to historic sites, and special commemorative projects on subjects like witchcraft and old anti-slavery days, the Society began to publish the *Danvers Historical Collections*, with its fascinating essays on local history.

In 1989, besides maintaining the Page House, this organization's properties include Tapley Memorial Hall, its museum and lecture hall; Glen Magna Farms with its mansion, McIntire-Derby summer house, magnificent

Before it became the property of the Danvers Historical Society in 1913, the Georgian style Page house was home to three generations of Pages. The builder was Col. Jeremiah Page who, as a militia captain, led his company to the Lexington Alarm in 1775.

The second owner, John Page, a brickmaker like his father, made most of the additions to his home: the extended parlor to the right, the piazza, and the conservatory. His daughter Anne, in the third generation, was an outstanding kindergarten teacher. It was

in the barn seen behind the house that she first taught local children their ABCs. For her contribution to the American kindergarten movement, Wellesley College named its early education center for her.

gardens, and the lattice-work gazebo replicated on its original site in 1988 as part of the Danvers Historical Society's centennial celebration.

All these achievements have resulted because a small group of dedicated local citizens set out a hundred years ago to honor their forebears.

Richard P. Zollo

Early in this century Salem photographer Frank Cousins took this photograph of the fireplace wall of the altered east parlor of the Page House. Here meetings of the Danvers Historical Society were once held. The delicate Federal mantel is overpowered by the dark, heavy pattern of the wallpaper and the massive Victorian sofa and piano.

Over the fireplace is a display of short- and cavalry swords. Framed military documents are hung to the left. Both Jeremiah Page and his son Samuel fought in the Revolutionary War. These documents are suspended from a late picture molding that has since been removed. Behind the raised-panel door to the right is a china closet.

A CHRONOLOGY OF EVENTS IN DANVERS, 1880-1910

Reprinted from the *Naumkeag Directory,* 1899 and 1912.

1880
June 19 Town voted to increase salaries of lady teachers.

1882
Sept. 12 Danvers Chorus Society formed.

1883
Jan. 5 Iron rolling mills burned.
Jan. 28 Fire destroyed shoe factory of Martin, Clapp & French, and three dwellings at Tapleyville.
Oct. 1 Dedication of remodeled town hall.

1884
May 3 Roller skating rink opened.
June 25 First horse cars from Salem.

1885
June 4 Mudge & Co.'s shoe factory burned; loss, $100,000.
July 9 First horse cars to Peabody.
July 30 Dedication of Rebecca Nourse monument.

1886
Feb. 2 Death of Hon. J. D. Philbrick, Boston Superintendent of schools.
July 24 Occupation of new police station.

1887
April 16 New England brick works burned; loss, $25,000.
April 16 Danvers Street Railway sold to Naumkeag St. Railway Co.
Sept. 7 First opening of Willard Home School for girls.
Dec. 17 Eightieth birthday of John G. Whittier celebrated.

1888
April 2 Danvers voted in favor of electric lighting, 212 to 6.
April 16 Town appropriated $15,000 for electric light plant.
June 2 First horse cars to Danvers Asylum.

1889
Jan. 2 First electric lights in streets.
Jan. 14 Burglary at F. Peabody's.
March New depot at Danversport completed.
June 6 Re-dedication of First Church.
July 22 Board of trade organized.
Oct. 31 Opening of Beverly and Danvers Street Railway.

1890
Jan. 1 Library of Danvers Historical Society dedicated.
Jan. 6 First late train from Boston.
Jan. 28 Fire destroyed First Church.
April 25 Celebration of Danvers Improvement Society. Governor and Lieut. Gov. present.

July 2 Fire destroyed Peabody Institute.
Sept. 15 Regular trips of Beverly and Danvers Street Railway to Plains.

1891
March 25 Co. K, 8th Regt., mustered in.
July 3 Burning of coal pockets at Beaver Brook.
Aug. 20 Sale of Spring estate to Xaverian Bros.
Aug. 22 Mrs. E. Duncan burned to death from explosion of oil stove.
Aug. 26 Dedication of armory.
Sept. 2 Dedication of new First Church.
Sept. 29 Parade of 8th Reg't; several soldiers injured.

1892
Feb. 3 Farwell's shoe factory burned; loss, $60,000.
Feb. 17 Meeting of Historical Society commemorative of witchcraft delusion of 1692.
March 29 Town seal adopted.
Sept. 7 Death of John G. Whittier, poet, at Hampton Falls.
Sept. 29 Arrival of new hook and ladder truck.
Oct. 10 Parade of temperance societies.
Oct. 19 New Peabody Institute dedicated.
Dec. 1 Electric cars from Salem.

1893
June 17 First electric cars to Asylum.

1894
Jan. 20 Red Men's hall burned.
April 11 Town authorized employment of superintendent of schools.
April 29 Buildings of J. C. Watson burglarized and burned.
June 30 Dedication of boulder on training field.
July 11 Burning of Danvers Iron Works.
Sept. 1 New school house dedicated at Danversport.
Oct. 1 Street car fares reduced.

1895
March 18 Town appropriated $3000 for electric fire alarm.
June 16 Citizens' mass meeting to act on Crane River nuisance.

1896
April 28 Burning of Hanson's grain mill.
Nov. 10 Col. Hutchinson monument dedicated.

1897
Feb. 17 William Kennedy sentenced to state prison for life for poisoning Learoyd family.
March 21 Martin & Co.'s shoe factory burned.
Aug. 6 Rubber works burned.

| Nov. 13 | New Tapley school house dedicated. |
| Nov. 25 | Fire at Bank building. |

1898

Feb. 1	Great blizzard and travel interrupted.
May 5	Co. K. 8th Regt. leaves for Camp Dewey.
Sept. 8	Visit of Rt. Hon. Joseph Chamberlain, British Colonial Secretary.
Nov. 23	Martin Kennedy shot by chief Bacon while robbing safe.

1899

| April 9 | Return of Co. K, 8th Regt. |
| April 11 | Parade and reception to Co. K, 8th Regt. |

1900

Jan. 2	Miss Maria Goodhue burned to death.
Mar. 29	Little Ruth Allen brutally assaulted.
April 8	John H. Barry fatally injured by colliding with an electric car.
May 6	Death of Hon. Wm. C. Endicott.
May 20	Dedication of Annunciation cemetery.
Oct. 11	Danvers Light Infantry disbanded.
Dec. 1	Postal sub-stations and free mail delivery established.

1901

Jan. 24	Poisoning of Samuel C. Putnam and family.
June 8	Formal opening of Danvers Country Club.
July 28	Death of Harriet Putnam Fowler.
Oct. 20	F. J. Derry's box factory and tenement house burned. Loss, $20,000.

1902

May 24	Street railroad extended to Country Club grounds.
June 15, 16, & 17	Notable celebration of 150th anniversary of incorporation of the town of Danvers.
Sept. 7	Death of Charles P. Kerans.
Nov. 7	Walter Farnum accidentally killed at Hood's Pond by two boys gunning.
Dec. 14	Fire at Martin Kelly Co.'s factory.

1903

Aug. 1	J. Pierpont Morgan guest of Gen. Francis Peabody.
Oct. 30	Horses in stable of B. W. Perry and others brutally treated by some unknown person.
Nov. 27	Collision of freight engines at Danvers Junction. Considerable damage.
Dec. 7	Stores in Tapleyville entered by desperate gang of burglars.

1904

| Jan. 26 | Station agent at Port attacked by three notorious yeggmen. |
| Nov. 14 | Death of Calvin Putnam, 89 years. |

1905

Jan. 9	Two cars derailed and considerably damaged at Eastern Division station.
Jan. 26	Two Danvers men sentenced for attempting bribery.
Feb. 9	Diphtheria epidemic at Port.
July 8	Charles P. Kerans plant totally destroyed by fire. Loss, $100,000.

1906

May 11	Ferncroft Inn totally destroyed by fire. Loss, $15,000.
May 15	Death of Rev. Alfred P. Putnam.
May 31	Water controversy between town of Danvers and D. I. H. [Danvers Insane Hospital] decided in favor of town.
June 18	Mailey child crushed in turntable at Eastern division station.
Sept. 26	Contract to build Waters River Bridge awarded to Pitman & Brown.
Oct. 12	Edson P. Pollard killed by live wire.
Nov. 1	Danvers Home for the Aged opened with five inmates.
Nov. 23	Appeal made to the public for funds to preserve the Rebecca Nourse house.

1907

Feb. 16	The Rebecca Nourse house purchased for preservation.
Sept. 10	St. John's School opened as preparatory college.
Dec. 10	Terrific explosion at electric light station.

1908

Feb. 24	$30,000 loss by fire at Martin Kelley & Co.'s factory.
April 21	Death of Martin Kelley.
June 18	Twenty-Third Street reopened by force.
Oct. 16	Louis Carbone, an Italian fruit dealer, brutally assaulted.

1909

Jan. 8	Electric car kills horse and demolishes a wagon.
June 10	E. B. Peabody assaulted by three men.
June 24	$15,000 fire at Ira Story factory.
Aug. 2	$3,000 fire in building of C. N. Perley, occupied by post office.

1910

Feb. 4	Death of Ira Story, aged 90.
Feb. 9	Danvers State Hospital for Insane quarantined on account of diphtheria.
Mar. 14	Resignations of Supt. Chas. W. Page and Dr. Chas. Richsher of Danvers State Hospital.
Apr. 25	Martin Kelley Co.'s shoe factory gutted by fire. Loss, $25,000.
Apr. 26	Death of William Penn Hussey.
Apr. 29	Death of Francis Peabody.
May 4	Insane murderers escaped from Danvers Asylum captured at Manchester, N. H.
May 5	Attendant at Danvers Insane Asylum arrested for aiding the escape of two inmates.
May 19	Daniel S. Doherty murdered his housekeeper and then committed suicide.
May 23	Horace S. Emerson loses his left hand in gearing of ice cream freezer.
July 10	Body of unknown man found in well on W. C. Endicott estate.
Nov. 26	Murder of Bertram W. Galloway by Chester W. Goodwin.

ACKNOWLEDGMENTS

We gratefully acknowledge the help and support of the following people and institutions in the production of this volume:

Photographic Credits: Danvers Archival Center, Danvers Historical Society, Margery Bockus, Margaret Crofts, Elizabeth Duffill, Essex Institute of Salem (Calvin Putnam Lumber Company, Formal Gardens at the State Hospital, Putnam's Sawmill, Western Division and Danversport Railroad Stations), Thomas Kerans, Carrie Kimball, Paul Littlewood, Leland Martin, Justin McCarthy, Jennie Morgan, Henrietta Sears, Richard Trask, and Richard Zollo.

Photographic Reproductions: Barry Kaplan, The Finer Image Photo Lab.

Danvers Historical Society Centennial Committee: Christine Patton, Chairman.

Centennial Book Committee: W. Keith Butler, Margaret Crofts, Brian Crowley, Kathie Farrell, Ann Jackson, Christine Patton, Joan Reedy, Richard Trask, Esther Usher, and Richard Zollo, Chairman.

Centennial Logo: Lynne Clarkin.

Marketing Committee: William Ardiff, Margaret Crofts, Elizabeth Duffill, Gordon Hamilton, Jr., Natalie Hamilton, Christine Patton, Betty Pennell, Geraldine Pugsley, Frederick Schaeffer, Marjorie Wetzel, W. Keith Butler, Chairman.

Proofreaders: Joan C. Butler and Virginia M. Zollo.

Typists: Ann Jackson and Mary Jane Wormstead.

Supporting Organizations: Danvers Archival Center, Danvers Historical Commission, Danvers Historical Society, Danvers Savings Bank, and the Peabody Institute Library of Danvers.

INTRODUCTION

As the twentieth century nears its conclusion, it is difficult for this generation of Americans to imagine our world in terms other than that of the pervasive visual images brought to us by the work of countless photographers and cameramen. Much of our knowledge and perception comes through the mass media's utilization of video tape, movie film, and still photography. Through these we witness wretched famine in Africa, cavorting penguins in the Antarctic, the sparkling lights of Paris, the magnificence of the Andromeda Galaxy, and the intricacies of the eye of a fly—all slices of reality which we as individuals could seldom behold as personal experiences.

In more personal terms, literally billions of pictures are taken by average Americans each year. Our generation has a myriad of light-captivating devices at our disposal: movie and video systems, box, instant, and disposable cameras, as well as sophisticated SLRs and larger format cameras. As a matter of cultural identity, we make numerous pictures of the mundane events and important milestones in our lives. Most families possess drawers and boxes filled with snapshots, slides, and movies of such scenes as a first birthday, a trip to Disney World, a backyard cookout, a deep snowstorm, or a wedding day. Photographic images are such an important part of our lives and culture that our remembered experiences are often taken, not from the mind's eye, but from our memory of what the pictures show. It would be difficult for us to visualize a world where photography did not exist.

To human history, however, photography is a recent blip on the time line. Though people from the earliest ages wanted a method to capture a transitory moment for later reflection, they were relegated through scores of generations to do so by describing it subjectively through the coordinated talents of eye, mind, and hand. Yet many attempted to find the technique which could entrap light and capture fleeting reality. The earliest known success in this quest was in 1827 when Joseph Niepce recorded on a

Pictorial representations of Danvers subjects prior to the invention of the camera are extremely limited. Abel Nichols (1815-1860) was a local artist of some note, and Maurice C. Oby (1824-1861) is known to have made pencil drawings of local scenes. Yet only a few score pre-1850 portraits of Danversites are known to exist, and fewer still are images of buildings and scenes. This 1836 engraving made for currency notes for the Village Bank represents the earliest known view of what was becoming Danvers' most prominent business district. The view is from High Street looking northeasterly towards Elm Street with (pictured from left) the Warren store, the Page house, Village Bank, Maple Street, Samuel Preston's house and shoe factory, and a part of the Berry Tavern complex.

pewter sheet a heliograph of a scene from a window at Le Gras, France. Following various experiments by many others, in 1839, Louis Daguerre, using a polished silver-coated copper sheet, a dark box with a simple lens, and various chemicals, demonstrated a fairly practical though unrushed method of capturing an image on a shiny plate. Daguerre remarked of his success, "I have seized the light, I have arrested its flight," and soon hundreds began utilizing his technology to produce tens of thousands of "daguerreotypes." Painted portraiture had been with us for centuries, but was available only to those few who could afford it and was only as accurate as the skill of the artist or inclination of the patron. It is not by chance that

the early daguerreotypes were mounted in ornately embossed cases and in intricate frames giving one an impression of a precious icon.

One must imagine the impact of our own times without photography to truly comprehend how this nineteenth-century photographic revolution brought about a new awareness and created such a wonder. For the first time in history average families could have and keep accurate images of a loved one who must travel far and long to earn a living, or of a child who died before its time. Images of the past could remain with the present forever!

As the nineteenth century continued, other photographic techniques were attempted, some improving

One of the earliest extant exterior views taken of Danvers is this ⅙ plate daguerreo-type. When processed by the photographer, the silver-coated copper plate acted as a mirror. The image itself was a direct positive and thus left and right are reversed to nature. Daguerreotypes had to be held at an angle to the light to overcome the mirror effect as well as the negative and positive elements inherent in the photographic image. This unique 1850s photograph shows a Concord-style coach with driver and two horses in front of the First Church (steps and corner of church at extreme right) on Centre Street. Behind the horses are the church's horse sheds with arch-trim doors, while behind the coach are glimpses of 39 and 35 Centre Street. The lettering on the side of the coach reads, "Tapleyville, Danvers & Salem." Daguerreotypes were in fashion between 1840 to about 1860. This coach line operated between 1849 and 1884.

Although today we are familiar with spot-news photos, during the early years of photography fleeting activity could not be captured on film. Yet, even given technical constraints of the era many old photographs do reveal poignant truths. This cased ferrotype portrait was made in 1861 of nineteen-year-old Nehemiah Putnam Fish, who enthusiastically enlisted in the Putnam Guards on July 5, 1861, to fight for the Union. Ferrotypes, often called tintypes, were direct positive images on a sheet of iron which had been lacquered black.

Three years later, this, a mounted albumen print made from a collodion wet-plate negative and referred to as a carte-de-visite, was taken of Fish. The contrast is striking. Fish had been captured in 1863 and held for four months at Libby Prison. Paroled, he had rejoined his company but was recaptured at Petersburg, Virginia, in June 1864. Again held in Rebel hands until parole, he was quickly discharged. Although lean when he enlisted, by the time this photograph was taken Fish's uniform hangs off the skeletally thin frame of a young man whose emaciated cheeks and hollow, staring eyes attest more graphically than words could ever do, the horrors of war. On August 9, 1864, Fish died from typhoid fever contracted while a prisoner.

Daguerre's process while others bloomed for a time to die soon after. Daguerreotypes, ambrotypes, and ferrotypes were popular for years as direct, one-image photographs. Negative-type films such as calotypes and collodion wet-plates were also developed allowing for multi-copies of the same image. About 1880, the gelatin dry-plate, a simple and more readily accepted negative system, was discovered followed later still by negative film in plastic rolls.

At first, images were chiefly made of rigid portraiture or still life, because of the length of the required exposure. By the turn of the century, though the bulk of photographic work was still formalized portrait images and scenic views, professionals and a growing number of amateur photographers, spurred on by simpler technologies, were creating more informal and candid photographs.

Danvers, Massachusetts, was a fair-size community of some four thousand inhabitants in 1855 primarily engaged in farming but also having some significant industry, including shoe manufacturing. During the 1850s and 1860s Danversites, like their Essex County neighbors, were having chronological progressions of formal portraits taken by daguerreotype and ambrotype artists at studios in Salem, Lynn, Beverly, and Boston. From the 1860s on, thousands of ferrotypes (tintypes), cartes-de-visite, and then cabinet-size pictures were created for purchase as keepsakes and photos of exchange, and many photograph albums were purchased in which to collect these massive numbers of portraits. Itinerant photographers would on occasion visit the smaller towns to make a photograph of a special local event or site.

Between 1880 and 1890 the number of professional photographers in the United States grew from ten thousand to twenty thousand, and it was during this period that in numerous smaller communities a professional photographer found it economically feasible to take up residence and establish a local studio. It was also during this time that amateur photography took on new meaning. Up until then, the relatively few serious amateurs who had to have a knack for the intricacies of the process were augmented, beginning in about 1889, by the rank amateurs. With their new Kodak box cameras they only needed to point and shoot. The company did the rest.

During this decade between 1880 and 1890 the population of Danvers grew from sixty-six hundred to seventy-five hundred. With few exceptions, most of what is known about professional Danvers photographers around the turn of the century comes to us from very brief references in local business directories or from hand-stamped artist identifications on the reverse of surviving photographs. Among those photographers active in Danvers at various times following the Civil War were O. H. Cook; William P. Fennessy, "landscape photographer" (circa 1890s); Elbridge Warren Merrill (early-to late-1890s); C. S. Neal, "Neal Brothers, Portobello Studio" (Circa 1900); W. Phippen (circa 1870); Charles W. Stiff, "photographer" (1870s); and E. C. Tibbetts (circa 1880s). Frank Cousins of Salem also did some Danvers souvenir photographic work in the 1890s though primarily of historic houses and sites.

By far the most influential photographer in Danvers at the turn of the century was Albert O. Elwell. Born in Gloucester in 1854, Elwell attended Holten High School in Danvers and became a photographic assistant at W. C. Hussey's studio in Salem and later at the Thompson studio in Amesbury. In 1887 Elwell moved back to Danvers and hired the top floor of the post office building at 9 Maple Street. An 1899 local publication stated of his thriving business, "His studio parlors and gallery are most thoroughly equipped with the most improved apparatus and appurtenances, elegantly furnished, tastefully arranged, accessible and attractive. Several assistants are employed and ladies find here every desirable accessory for proper posing, and are invariably pleased with the work done." Elwell referred to himself as an "Artist-Photographer" and it was commented of him, "His facilities for the production of pastels, water-colors and landscapes are unsurpassed." By 1902 Elwell had left Danvers, and in 1912 William Taylor, a portrait and commercial photographer, took up residence in town working from Elwell's former address. Salem photographer Joseph F. Briggs became a Danvers resident in 1911, and by about 1916 procured Taylor's business and served the photographic needs of the community for the next few decades.

The approximately two hundred photographs chosen for inclusion in this publication represent the work of Elwell, Merrill, and other professional Danvers and area photographers, as well as a sampling of the work of a number of amateurs most of whose identities are unknown.

Many of the photographs represent formalized scenes and staged events because of the nature of nineteenth-century photography and the tastes of the period. Some of these photographs were for the souvenir trade and meant to instill local pride and identity, while others were taken by amateurs with hand-held cameras used in a more intimate and informal setting. The editors of this book were limited by what photographs of this era survive and which would reproduce for the greatest clarity and sharpness. Yet even with these restraints a casual examination of the contents will show a rich, though somewhat limited, view of Danvers at the turn of the century.

Almost the instant a photograph is snapped, it becomes a document of history and, if examined carefully, can tell the viewer a significant amount about the subject captured on the photograph and the time in which it was taken. To be truly appreciated, photographs must be understood in the context of their time and with a critical understanding of their technical and cultural limitations. Black and white photography is not a picture of true reality, but rather an intepretation of the reality of unregistered colors of light waves. Looking upon images of the nineteenth century, we must remind ourselves that that century was not colored black and white, or sepia. The medium upon which an image was made also skews our view of the reality of the event being photographed, be it

During the 1880s and 1890s, the most popular mode of photographic portraiture was thin albumen paper prints mounted on cards in forms typically larger than the earlier popular carte-de-visite size. Victoria (3¼" x 5") and Boudoir (5¼" x 8½") were two of the standard size picture cards, though the Cabinet style (4½" x 6¼") was the most popular. This cabinet photograph is of Nellie May Withey. Born on May 3, 1887, to Charles and Lillian (Esty) Withey, Nellie was dressed in her finest clothes for a visit to the local photographer. A heavy cord tied around her robe, the small bunch of flowers, and the pouting face are captured along with the less prominent photographer's painted background flat and artificial grass and rock props, all making a fine visual rememberance of Nellie for her family to treasure. The photographer usually had his card stock printed or embossed with his name and address as a reminder for print re-orders, or as an incentive to other possible clients.

of the pristine grainlessness of a daguerreotype plate or the tonal differences among present-day color film dyes. Photographs, particularly staged photographs, must be looked at critically, understanding that they can distort, simplify, or misrepresent reality by the photographer including or excluding items or pointing the camera in a certain direction to the exclusion of other directions. Thus, as you examine the photographs within this collection, look not only with a curiosity of how it was in years gone by, but also examine the not-so-obvious aspects of the photograph and know that as in all other historical pursuits, the study of photographic documentation does not reveal "the" truth and reality, but rather "a" truth and reality.

Richard B. Trask

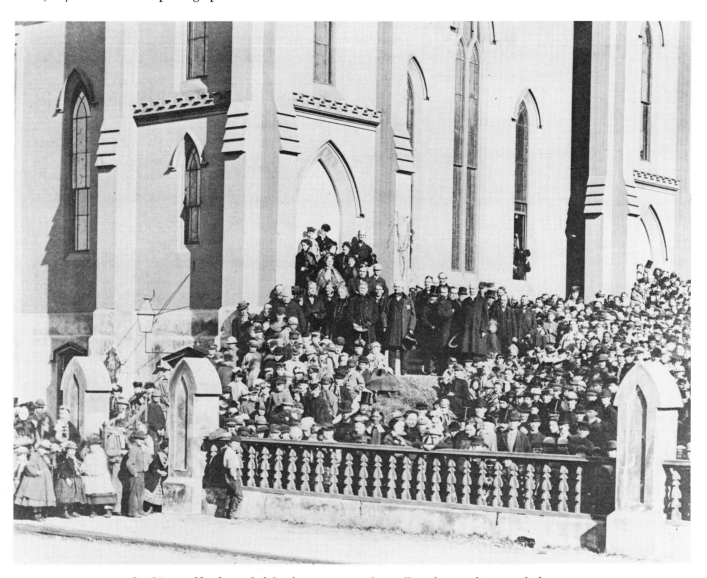

In 1867 noted banker and philanthropist George Peabody made an infrequent visit from London to his native town. On April 13, Peabody was feted at various ceremonies including a reception by Danvers school children at the Universalist Church on High Street. This resulting picture, made from a collodian wet-plate negative, was described a few days later in the South Danvers Wizard: "The reception was a most decided success in all its parts. Its out-of-door features are sure to be perpetuated by the excellent photographic view which was taken of the multitude in front of the church by Mr. Stiff. Everything about the work combined to secure a perfect picture. The sun was bright and clear, the grouping was good, the people were still and quiet, and the instrument and chemicals must have been in working order. The result is very gratifying to Mr. Peabody who pronounced it to be the best work of the kind he has seen, whether in this country or Europe."

Park Street and Back Bay, circa 1900.

❧ THEIR HOMES ❧

As Danvers moved through the social, economic, and political changes of the turn of the century, one of the few constants in townspeople's lives was the dominance of the home. It was the focus of everyday life—the place where most were born and died, the source of strongest personal ties, the nurturer of deepest-held ideas. Indeed it can be defined by all the intangible qualities that we say "make a house a home." But in order to approach Danvers' past, we must learn about the houses to understand the homes. An examination of the buildings, the furnishings, and other properties with which people surrounded themselves provides insight into the times. By 1900, houses in Danvers represented the many styles that had come and gone in over two hundred years, and a wide spectrum of types, from the very modest cottage to the grandest mansion.

The variety of house styles that were then in Danvers represented the cultures of the periods in which they were made—not only the materials, technologies, and tastes of the times, but also the values, philosophies, and expectations of society. The earliest Danvers homes linked English and medieval traditions with the new materials and demands of the New World. Characterized by massive chimneys, pegged frames, and sloping lean-tos (usually added later), these structures established patterns on which later building traditions are based. New styles developed over time, though not with clearly visible breaks in periods. The eighteenth century brought the Georgian style, with its strict symmetry, pedimented center entry, and classical details. It remained long in fashion, and Danvers' high-style eighteenth-century houses are Georgian—Page House, Reverend Wadsworth's house, and The Lindens. Elements common to these are found also in the classical style that followed Georgian—Adam or Federal. High-style Federal found expression more commonly in Salem, Massachusetts; in Danvers, houses were less grand, but were built with at least some elements of the new fashion, such as fanlights over the entry. Architectural details were more delicate than in Georgian styles, though the symmetry and classicism remained.

Both the Georgian and Adam styles in America followed closely the designs of England. In the years after the War of 1812, Americans rejected English architectural influence in favor of a new revival style that seemed especially appropriate to the new republic. The Greek Revival style proclaimed American succession to the spirit of Ancient Greece and its democratic ideals. In homage to Greek temples, houses and other buildings featured pedimented gables, bold moldings, columns, and a coat of white paint. Greek Revival stayed in fashion and by the mid-century was one of several popular styles for homes. As romanticism took hold on American cultural life, use of romantic styles in buildings increased. Gothic Revival symbolized the perceived virtues of the Middle Ages. With a popularity paralleled by a taste for Sir Walter Scott, Gothic Revival used steeply pitched roofs, decorated vergeboards, and pointed arches to evoke a sense of the medieval past. Romanticism inspired another style of the mid-century, the Italianate. An interpretation of northern Italian farmhouses, the style was adaptable to the elaborate or the restrained, and featured low-pitched roof, wide overhanging eaves with decorative brackets, and tall, round-headed windows.

Enthusiasm for other styles arose after the Civil War, along with new building techniques and mass-production of house components. The renovation of Paris by Napoleon III inspired the Second Empire style in America. Its salient feature was the mansard roof. Used in Danvers in many one-story workers' houses, mansard roofs created a full usable story out of attic space. The Stick style, like Gothic Revival, was an adaptation of medieval building traditions. Intersecting boards applied over clapboarding were supposed to have represented the inner structure of the house, but were, in fact, pure decoration that had no relation to the balloon-frame construction underneath. Queen Anne style also drew inspiration from the Middle Ages and called for an interplay of textures, materials, and colors on wall surfaces. Towers, turrets, and bays contributed to its exuberant asymmetry. Toward the end of the century, domestic architecture was still looking backward in time, though not quite so far as to medievalism. With a post-Centennial enthusiasm for the classical forms of colonial and early republican America, Colonial Revival combined Georgian, Federal, and contemporary elements of style. It suited Danvers well, a town that at the turn of the twentieth century retained a fair amount of the built environment it had at the turn of the nineteenth.

Historic Danvers

During the middle years of the nineteenth century a number of Danvers residents began to be aware and collect accounts and stories of the history and development of their town. In 1848 Reverend J. W. Hanson published the first history of Danvers, the volume running some three hundred pages. It was not until after the nation's centennial in 1876, however, that a wave of popular interest in local history washed over much of the country. The Danvers Historical Society was established in 1889 and during the 1890s handsome local booster and newspaper publisher Frank E. Moynahan printed two separate booklets containing historical sketches of the town and including numerous photographs, facts, and traditions concerning the most obvious surviving artifacts of the past—its old houses. Around the turn of the nineteenth century, Danvers had a fine collection of seventeenth and eighteenth-century dwellings, many still in use as family farms. These ancient houses and their stories gave the town a unique identity and source of pride, and numerous photographers, both professional and amateur, made views of these dwellings for distribution as souvenirs or as personal keepsakes.

Traditionally dating to the 1660s, this house, known as the Rea-Putnam-Fowler house, is located at 111 Locust Street some distance from the road. Houses dating prior to about 1725 are today referred to as "First Period" structures. This one exhibits a slanting "salt-box" roof, an eighteenth-century "sentry box" front entry, and though difficult to pick out in this circa 1895 photograph by Frank Cousins, a curved plaster coving on the front roof line at the eaves. Edmund Putnam added the east side of the house about 1758. A tailor and farmer, Putnam was also captain of an alarm company which responded to the Lexington Alarm in April, 1775. A convert to Universalism, in 1829 Putnam hosted the first meeting of the new society at his home. A later resident here was Augustus Fowler, a noted local naturalist and ornithologist who died at the homestead in 1894.

The Prince-Osborn house is pictured here on its original Spring Street location. Built circa 1670 the lefthand side of the main house shows the remnants of a front overhang. The original owner of the house was Robert Prince. On his death, the property was divided between his two sons—James, six years old, and Joseph, two. Their mother Sarah, who continued to live here, created a scandal by bringing an indentured servant, Alexander Osborne, to live with her. They eventually married, but resentment continued to exist in the neighborhood. On February 29, 1692, a warrant was sworn out against a bed-ridden Sarah as a witch. Before she went to trial, however, she died in a Boston prison on May 10. Daniel Cahill purchased the house from St. John's Normal College and had it moved to 273 Maple Street in 1915, at which time its "broken-back" lean-to section was removed.

This 1885 photograph is of 171 Holten Street, one of the town's most historic structures. Initially built in about 1670, this house has undergone additions in 1689, 1700, 1750, and 1832 making it a fine example of chronological house develop-ment. This was the 1692 home of Sarah Holten, who gave damaging testimony against Rebecca Nurse during the witchcraft hysteria. In the mid-eighteenth century it was the residence of Dr. Samuel Holten. Holten held numerous elective and appointive governmental positions including serving as a member of the Continental Congress and being a signer of the Articles of Confederation in 1778. In 1921 the local Daughters of the American Revolution acquired the house as its meeting place.

The graceful plastered coving (a foil for the straightback salt-box roofline), the large pilastered chimney, the multi-light windows, and the awkward nineteenth-century sentry box entryway, made this one of the area's most architecturally interesting houses. This dwelling was built for Deacon Benjamin Putnam prior to 1700. Located on North Street, the house burned to the ground the night of January 2, 1900. Old, feeble, and eccentric Maria Goodhue lost her life in the conflagration. Because the house was enveloped in flames when neighbors rushed to the scene, the fire company was not even called out because no source of water was nearby. A local newspaper speculated about murder and robbery and even the possibility that Miss Goodhue had set the fire herself as she had told neighbors that burning was the best way to die. But the cause of the fire was never determined. The next day strangers were seen sifting through the ruins for possible treasure the eccentric spinster was rumored to have hidden away.

As was typical of most rural "First Period" houses, this dwelling located at 182 Centre Street faced south for best advantage of the winter sunlight even though the front of the house faced away from the street. Built about 1726, this was the Elisha Hutchinson house and the birthplace of local military hero Israel Hutchinson. The house is unusual in that it survives as an example of a "half house" and as originally built included only two rooms and a chimney on the left side. Some time after 1780, the lean-to and jog were added and at a later time the original chimney was moved. The house, unlike most in the area, never had the parlor side of the structure added. Off to the side is a shingled barn, and in the background at 191 Centre Street one can see the Mudge-Pratt house and its extensive outbuildings.

The Putnam house on Maple Street near the junction of Route 1 has been in the possession of the same family since its construction. Though the original section of this house was traditionally built in 1648 for Thomas Putnam, his grandson David built the Georgian style gambrel roof portion intersecting the old. This section is most prominent in this circa 1897 photograph. The most famous occupant of the dwelling was Israel Putnam, who was born here in 1718 and spent his early years on this farm. "Old Put," as the general was affectionately called by his troops, held a well-earned reputation for bravery. He fought with the Rangers in the French and Indian War and commanded the American troops at Bunker Hill. Putnam's exploits gave him a status of folk hero during the late eighteenth into the nineteenth century. An 1897 Daughters of the American Revolution plaque noting the birthplace of Israel Putnam can be seen attached to the house.

The Col. Jesse Putnam house was built circa 1750 near present Route 95 on Old Maple Street and is an example of "double" house construction. In the War of 1812, Putnam commanded an artillery company of the state militia. Unusual to Danvers, but not unique, is the roof of the house which is gambrel on the south face and a combination of gambrel and lean-to on the back. A balustrade ran around the gambrel portion of the roof. Although the rear sentry box vestibules were almost identical, the front entrances were quite different. The attached outbuildings are at a right angle to the house, the barn dating to 1831. Note the variety of fencing about the property.

Majestic elms shade the house, and a nearby stream once flowed into what the neighborhood children called Turtle Pond, which was the Colonel's source for ice. The Danvers State Hospital looms in the background atop Hathorne Hill. The house, always occupied by members of the same family, burned in the 1950s.

This Georgian gable-on-hip roof house located at 73 Centre Street was built in 1785 for Benjamin Wadsworth, minister of the First Church. Originally possessing twelve over twelve light window sashes, in 1881 these old-style windows were changed "to the modern pattern," destroying its architectural purity and classic look in exchange for prevalent fashion. This 1891 photograph includes residents (from left) Sarah, Frank, and Bertha Wilkins standing by the dirt walk. Though the old windows are gone, the formal front pedimented entry with its fluted pilasters, five-light transom, eight-panel door, and dentil molding show this as a classical example of its style. In 1983, the original style windows were reinstated throughout the house.

Estates

The first few wealthy citizens to establish country estates in Danvers were late eighteenth-century East India merchants, shipbuilders, and owners of fishing fleets in Salem and Marblehead. While they set their mansions for the best views and best air and did some landscaping, they thought primarily of their properties as farms that would be sources of fresh produce and sanctuaries from the summer's heat—and sometimes the intrigues of commerce and politics.

Nineteenth-century estate holders—distinguished jurists, financiers, manufacturers, and merchants—bought up old farms and hired professional gardeners to beautify their acres. Following the English custom, they gave their estates names like Elmhurst, Fairchance, Hampstead, and Maplewood.

Among the most important Danvers estates were the three featured here: Oak Knoll, Glen Magna, and The Lindens. The first was the home of the poet John Greenleaf Whittier during much of the last sixteen years of his life. Its owners, the poet's cousins, furnished it more simply than the other two because they were Quakers.

Glen Magna was known to three generations of Peabody-Endicott owners as simply The Farm. William C. Endicott, the Younger, in the fourth generation called it Glen Magna after the place in Leicestershire, England, from which the Endicotts emigrated.

Finally there was The Lindens built by Marblehead merchant Robert Hooper, a Tory during the Revolution. It had great architectural distinction. Sold at auction in 1937, it was taken down board by board and re-erected on Kalorama Road in Washington, D.C. Its removal was an irreplaceable loss to the town.

The only Danvers estate known throughout the English-speaking world was Oak Knoll, where the poet Whittier received such prominent writers and reformers as Oliver Wendell Holmes, Sarah Orne Jewett, Dorothea Dix, and Paul Hamilton Hayne. Built in 1842 as a summer home for William Lander of Salem, the salmon-colored Oak Knoll had grounds laid out on principles set down by Andrew Jackson Downing, America's first landscape gardener. The Greek Revival mansion had a partially enclosed facade with two open verandas, each supported by two Doric columns. Seen here on the east veranda is the poet with his cousins, the Johnson sisters, and little Phoebe Woodman, the adopted daughter of Abby (Johnson) Woodman.

During John Greenleaf Whittier's sixteen-year sojourn at Oak Knoll starting in 1876, he was the Dean of American letters and one of the country's best-loved poets. Not well educated, but an avid reader, the poet had used as his model the Scottish writer Robert Burns. Willing to sacrifice his literary gifts for a cause, Whittier, an abolitionist, strove for years before the Civil War to liberate the slaves. So associated with the Northeast was he that New England settlers travelling west in covered wagons carried his works with them as reminders of home. Most of the over one hundred poems he composed after his seventieth birthday were written here at Oak Knoll. In 1960, the home he made famous was razed to make room for a housing development.

Whittier's "den" contained pictures of his friends Emerson, Longfellow, and Senator Charles Sumner and favorite White Mountain scenes. The picture to the right of Jefferson's over the fireplace is of the Brazilian emperor, Dom Pedro II, who had translated some of Whittier's anti-slavery poems into Portuguese. On top of the bookcase on the right are the stuffed remains of two of the poet's pets—Davey, the mockingbird, and Friday, the squirrel. After their deaths, he could not bear to part with them. While he is little read today in schools, older readers seeing the Maltese crosses in the carpet may be reminded that more than twenty hymns sung in churches have lyrics taken from his verses, the most familiar being "Dear Lord and Father of Mankind."

This view of Glen Magna was taken in 1892 and shows what the mansion looked like after Joseph Peabody, a wealthy Salem merchant, remade the farmhouse he had purchased from Capt. Jonathan Ingersoll in 1814. While this side was the main approach, the garden entrance was more elaborate. Spread out before its veranda was the garden planned by George Heussler, an Alsatian landscape gardener who worked for Joseph Peabody. To the left is a huge barn, since levelled, that gave the name "The Farm" great accuracy.

Handsomely remodeled and enlarged by the architectural firm of Little, Brown, and Moore for Ellen Peabody Endicott and her son William, this is the Glen Magna mansion visitors have seen since 1893. A third floor was added over the central portion with its new, elegant two-story pedimented portico and its great Doric columns. The balustrade there and around the wings, the Palladian window, the Chippendale-style railings that surround excavated areas in front of both wings (to give more sunlight to the basement) are all popular features of the Colonial Revival style. The small structure to the left is the laundry, called by William their Petit Trianon. The trees in tubs were removed in winter, not to an orangery, but to a plain New England greenhouse.

Ellen (Peabody) Endicott is seated beneath the portrait of her beautiful daughter Mary. Joseph Peabody was the first owner of the estate; the second was George Peabody, his son; and third was Ellen Endicott, George's daughter. Ellen became the wife of William C. Endicott, Secretary of War in Grover Cleveland's first administration. Ellen's son was known as William C. Endicott, the Younger. He was the family historian. His sister Mary met her first husband, the Right Honorable Joseph Chamberlain, then British Colonial Secretary, in Washington. After his death, she married Canon William Carnegie, dean of Westminster Abbey and house chaplain to Parliament.

"Chintzy" is an easy adjective to describe this room, "Grandpa Peabody's parlor," in 1892. It has the pleasing informality of a country home. While there are elegant pieces here like the convex mirror over the fireplace, there are also country pieces like the painted Windsor rocking chair. The fancy Sheraton side chairs and the other furniture set against the walls constitute an arrangement out of style at the time. The center table is in the later Victorian mode as is the lamp above it. This room, known to the Endicotts also as the small parlor, remained essentially untouched structurally after the remodelling.

The 1793 Federal-style McIntire summer or tea house was the reason for this estate's survival. Designed by woodcarver and architect Samuel McIntire for Elias Hasket Derby, once the richest of Salem's merchants, it adorned Derby's summer property in South Danvers, now Peabody. In 1901, Ellen Endicott had the fragile structure moved to Glen Magna. This 1904 view shows the tea house minus later flanking lattice-work fences. Louise Thoron Endicott, William's widow, died in 1958 leaving the building to the Danvers Historical Society, but without the ground on which it stood. In a bold, cooperative effort, the estate was purchased in 1963 by the Society and the town of Danvers. The Society's portion was the eleven-acre central section with the mansion and gardens in the midst of which was the summer house.

Joseph Chamberlain planned this flower garden in 1893. The sundial was a copy of one belonging to Governor John Endecott. The original stood at his Orchard Farm on the banks of Waters River. Of greatest interest in the photograph is the rustic bench. On his 1893 visit to the estate, Chamberlain was protected by bodyguards disguised as farmers and herdsmen. Because of his stand in Parliament against home rule for Ireland, he was extremely unpopular. One evening as the couple sat close together on this bench, a gunman, hidden in the bushes nearby, took aim at Chamberlain, but did not fire for fear of hitting Mary. He was captured the following morning, and the couple left immediately, not wishing to upset Mary's aged parents who were not made aware of what had happened. An account of this is related in Diana Laing's Mistress of Herself.

Probably the greatest architectural loss to Danvers was The Lindens, the summer residence of Marblehead merchant Robert Hooper. The Georgian style, 1754, gambrel-roofed dwelling built on Sylvan Street included a wooden simulated ashlar finish on the front elevation, quoins, monumental Corinthian columns, and a balustrade on the upper slope. The house was used as official residence for Governor Thomas Gage, commander-in-chief of British forces in North America, during his stay in the summer of 1774 when the capital of Massachusetts was shifted from Boston to Salem. Known as The Lindens because those trees lined the avenue leading to the mansion, the summer estate belonged in the last half of the nineteenth century to Francis Peabody, who entertained here, among other famous people, George Peabody, the international banker and philanthropist.

It is difficult to believe that this room in The Lindens is part of the interior of an eighteenth-century American manor house. It is certainly rich enough with its dark panelling; heavy, carved Jacobean-style furniture; and sumptuous pillows and fabrics to have impressed J. Pierpont Morgan, the international banker who was an occasional guest, just as Francis Peabody was a guest aboard Morgan's yacht The Corsair. The crests on the chairs in the room are appropriate for someone who probably considered himself part of an American aristocracy. Francis Peabody lived at The Lindens summers for fifty years (1860-1910) and took an active part in local affairs.

"Fine example of high-post bedstead" is written on the mat to which this circa 1910 photograph of a chamber at The Lindens is attached. Set on the bed's sturdy Marlborough legs are delicately reeded posts supporting an arched canopy. Pattern on pattern dominates the room. Oriental rugs are laid over the heavily patterned carpeting. Chintz covers the chair and the canopy with its three swags. The chair has an unusual number of linen antimacassars. Ribbons tie up the striped curtains on the bed, and another ribbon is tied to the handle of the bed warmer. This ostentatious room represents a romanticized, turn-of-the-century idea of a colonial chamber for someone wealthy enough, like Robert Hooper its builder, to have been called "King."

House Portraits

One of the most popular and widely used photographic set pieces during the second half of the nineteenth century was that of the owners posing in front of their homes. By including family members, hired help, family pets, and vehicles these pictures made for the family a most personal remembrance, as well as visual proof of outward stability, success, and pride.

———————————— ————————————

All eyes at the Dr. Jesse Snow residence at 141 Holten Street gaze towards the photographer's lens located across the street in this circa 1867 photograph. The 1855 Gothic Revival house replete with intricately cut-out vergeboards and vertical board-and-batten siding, fancy fencing, well-kept grounds, and a cupola-topped barn is the backdrop for assorted fancy-dressed family members. Two hired help hold the reins of family horses. The picture records that this is obviously the home of a successful man.

Just as proud but not nearly so rich as Dr. Snow, farmer Daniel C. Roberts, smoking a clay pipe, poses in front of his early "First Period" style house at 35 Centre Street with its more recent Greek Revival front entry. An examination of this 1891 photograph records a woman, possibly Roberts's wife Elizabeth, just visible in the open first floor window. A "Beverly projection" entry is attached to the opposite side of the house, while a large barn and additional outbuilding are glimpsed at the rear. The grounds are unkempt and include a worn board fence.

Samuel Page Fowler stands by the side porch of his circa 1844 residence at 12 Cherry Street along with other members of the family and the pet cat (sitting on the porch steps). This circa 1880 photograph highlights typical features of the locally built Greek Revival style house including a front entry with pilasters, an entablature, sidelights, and transom. Popular nationwide between 1820 and 1860, more houses were built in this style in Danvers proportionate to the population than any other architectural style before or perhaps since. Fowler was a remarkable multifaceted citizen active in the religious and political life of Danvers, as well as being a noted amateur naturalist and antiquarian. Fowler died at his home in 1888.

Successful Danversport grocer Aaron W. Warren stands in his formal best with wife Hannah and daughter Anna before their Italianate style house at 149 High Street in this circa 1866 photograph. The house includes projecting roof cornices, paired brackets, and a flatboard front elevation on this 1860 dwelling. Fencing was an important property feature for any home, as it separated public and private space. The turned post in the middle of the walkway kept large animals from wandering onto the property, and the elegance of the fence diminishes as it runs beyond the front yard.

Though brick manufacturing was a major
industry in Danvers, few local dwellings
were constructed of the material. One exception was the William Endicott house on
Water Street built in a simplified Italianate
style. Born in 1809 into a family of sea-
farers, Endicott was shipwrecked in 1831 in
the Fiji Islands and lived to tell stories of his
experiences with cannibals. An ardent abolitionist, Endicott by the time this photograph
was taken in the 1870s, was an inspector in
the Salem Customhouse.

This "French Cottage" was built about 1876 by local contractor Nathan T. Putnam and exhibits wooden corner quoins, brackets, and two styles of roof tiles. The dwelling is similar to numerous mansard-roofed Second Empire style structures built in Danvers. Members of the Thomas Sylvester Trask family pose in this circa 1890 photograph made by A. O. Elwell. Trask was a painter and his work wagon carries the lettering on the side "House Painting."

Recently wed Mr. and Mrs. Willis Munsey (third and fourth from left) stand in front of their 1894 Queen Anne style house at 40 Centre Street in this circa 1905 photograph. A milk dealer by trade, Munsey, his father William, and driver Michael Whelan are decked out in ties, soft workmen's caps, and overalls. Their close-sided milk wagon is nearby in the drive.

❧ THEIR ECONOMY ❧

In 1899 the book *Danvers, Massachusetts*, "published in the interest of the Town by the *Danvers Mirror*," put forth the industrial ethic of the time. In describing a town whose economy relied on farming, commerce, and industry, the book makes one reference to farming, and this under the heading "MANUFACTURING":

> Agriculture would seem to have been the primal industry which occupied Danvers' first settlers; but she unquestionably owes the growth of the past years to the introduction of manufactures....[A] town so well located as Danvers should invite capital to be invested in manufacturing.

Danvers devoted large tracts of its acreage to agriculture, but town promoters labelled the pursuit "primal." Most of the nation believed that the key to the common welfare was in vigorous industrialization. The process created forces both constructive and destructive, and changed irrevocably the character of the economy and society.

Frank E. Moynahan, publisher of *Danvers, Massachusetts*, took pains to assure his readers:

> Among the intelligent and well meaning manufacturers and merchants of Danvers the spirit of public and commercial progress is strongly developed, and among these that feeling of unity of thought and action so absolutely necessary to individual and collective welfare is most strikingly displayed.

Indeed if anything were strikingly displayed, it was change. Shoe factories—C. C. Farwell & Co., G. A. Creighton & Son, Eaton & Armitage, Martin Kelley, Clapp & Tapley, J. W. Tulloch, Donovan & Shea; the Danvers Iron Works; tanneries—Barnard, Friedman & Co., Naumkeag Leather, Plumer and Kerans; Colcord-Richardson machine shop; lumbermills—Woodman Bros. & Ross, Calvin Putnam; Lore & Russell coal company; Massachusetts Glove Company. These were among the industries of turn-of-the-century Danvers. The growing economy furnished jobs to more and more people—people from surrounding farms or from other countries. The emphasis was on productivity, efficiency, and profit.

Transportation and communication also underwent revolution.

> The growth of any community is greatly enhanced by the extent and liberal character of its transportation facilities. Few towns in the commonwealth are better provided with railroad facilities both for shipping and for passenger traffic than Danvers.

Moynahan then described the Boston and Maine railroad and its nine stations in town, and the street railway system of electric roads and half-hourly service to other towns. The Postal and Western Union telegraph companies and the New England Telegraph Company "place[d] Danvers in direct communication with the entire world." The rapid spread of transportation and communication networks inexorably drew Danvers outside of itself. It came in contact with and became itself an increasingly consumer-oriented society.

Mass production and mass marketing created goods that never before had been available, or at least not to the average Danversite. An 1899 photograph of the interior of J. O. Perry's market reveals rows and rows of canned goods. Though the process had been invented early in the century, canning was not practical for the market until the 1880s when machines mass-produced tin-plate cans. The average daily diet improved as many theretofore regional foods were preserved and widely distributed. Another 1899 interior photograph shows W. C. Nickerson's clothing store, displaying stacks and stacks of trousers, shirts, socks, and suspenders. Ready-made clothing, a rarity at mid-century, was commonplace by century's close, and most people could afford to buy their clothes "off the rack." "Nickerson's store enjoyed such stock turnover that out-of-style clothing did not accumulate on his shelves and tables." It was a feature important to note for a population increasingly concerned with style.

America was changing from an agrarian to an industrial nation. The change meant, among other things, that more and more people worked away from the home and farm, that a growing transportation and communication network widened hometown connections with a larger society, and that a new and ever-changing standard of living quickly converted luxuries into everyday things. Danvers felt the effects.

Farming

The Danvers area was originally referred to simply as The Farms. In the second quarter of the seventeenth century, men who had land here would row out in their shallops from Salem Town to till their fields by day and then return in the evening for safety.

On Orchard Farm, the 1632 land grant given to John Endecott, fruit trees and other cuttings from England flourished. And in the eighteenth century, because corn was the main crop in the region, gristmills were important to the local economy. For that reason New Mills (Danversport) was first settled to take advantage of tidal power.

In his history of Danvers, J. W. Hanson listed the crops raised in 1848: corn, rye, barley, oats, potatoes, onions, and squash. Butter, cheese, honey, beef, and pork were all sent to market. Fairs sponsored annually by the Essex County Agricultural Society were sometimes held in the fields behind the Berry Tavern. Here Danvers-made plows and other farm implements were exhibited. Local farmers like Francis Dodge, Perley Goodale, Charles P. Preston, Elijah Pope, and Orrin Putnam took prizes in various categories ranging from ploughing with double team to June butter.

In 1888, Alden P. White, in his account of the town for a history of Essex County, noted, "The land here is rich and level, and every acre is worked for all it is worth." Hundreds of barrels of onions were raised each year within half a mile of The Lindens. Indeed, the Danvers carrot and the Danvers onion became popular varieties across the country. Jonathan Perry, a Danvers farmer, was credited with being the first farmer in Essex County to raise strawberries for market. In addition, according to White, "No town in the State is so distinguished for its superior orcharding."

Photographer Frank Cousins captured this pastoral scene in the 1890s standing on Hobart Street looking across a field being harrowed. In 1692 members of the First Church of Salem Village that stood near the stone-wall in the foreground felt considerably harrowed themselves by the witchcraft delusion that broke out in their midst. Whipple Hill is in the background. Missing from the hill and most of the landscape are hard-wood trees like oaks and maples. The region had been so denuded by the demand for wood that in the 1840s a concerted effort was made regionally to exhort communities and invididuals to plant trees. For this reason Danvers streets like Maple, Locust, Pine, and Oak were named to encourage householders to plant the appropriately named trees for the roads on which they lived.

This photograph of the Nurse house and its outbuildings surrounded by the openness of fields was taken in 1891. It was from here in the tense days of 1692 that Rebecca Nurse was seized by the authorities to be imprisoned, tried, and hanged as a witch. In the center of the picture is the wellhouse and to its right can be seen the barn and two corn cribs. At the turn of the nineteenth century other outbuildings might have included an ice-house and a peat shed. Like most Danvers farms, this one was then engaged in market gardening and included an orchard. The Nurse homestead was purchased in 1907 by a local preservation group, thus becoming the first historic property to be saved and restored in Danvers. In 1981, the Danvers Alarm List Company acquired the property and developed it as a homestead museum.

This salt-box roof house with side "Beverly projection" was the circa 1654 home of George Jacobs, who was accused of practicing witchcraft and executed on August 19, 1692. The two cows grazing in this 1890 photograph were part of a large herd, for this was a dairy farm operated at the time by William Jacobs. He, like other farmers, recognized their declining influence nationally together with what they perceived to be a loss of traditional family values that to them the farm families exemplified. In 1902 local farmers organized Danvers Grange No. 263 and contributed generously to home and community projects with funds raised at fairs and bazaars. When the Improvement Society gave the town Danvers Park in 1913, Grange member Otis Verry contributed approximately seventy trees for its beautification.

In 1792, Elias Endicott built the handsome farmhouse, pictured here on the left, a year after his marriage to Nancy Cressy of Beverly. Besides being a farmer raising sheep, vegetables, and fruit, Endicott was a tanner, currier, and shoemaker. His three daughters—Mary, Clarissa, and Nancy—went through all the steps of converting wool from raw to finished products. Much sought-after dressmakers, they could also prepare their flax to make linen. These women could even weave some of the grasses growing on the farm into straw bonnets. From native plants like crocuses, they made their own dyes. The building facing the camera was probably Endicott's shoe factory. In 1955 the farmhouse was carefully dismantled before the area was flooded for the Putnamville reservoir and re-erected out of town.

The Mudge-Pratt farmhouse at 191 Centre Street was built circa 1805 by Simon Mudge, Sr. Capt. Amos Pratt, an officer in a local artillery company who married Almira Mudge, purchased the farm from his brother-in-law William in 1856. The small building with the chimney next to the barn had a shoemaker's shop on the second floor. Note the milk pails drying in the clean air. The forty-by-fifty-foot barn was built in 1876. From its cupola, one could see Abbot Hall in Marblehead. The air-stacked wood in the foreground was probably posts for making split-rail fences. Pratt raised fruits and vegetables for city markets—apples (mostly Baldwins), peas, potatoes, onions, and "pickles." Pratt also owned a twenty-acre woodlot and a share in a peat bog in Middleton.

Although it is unknown which barn interior
this is in Danvers, we do know the photograph was taken around 1895 by E. W.
Merrill. Farm scenes, particularly interior
views, are quite rare because they were so
unremarkably normal, and thus not worthy
of a photograph. Here in the whitewashed
interior two cows stand in their stalls, while
chickens peck on the barn floor. Hay is
stored in the loft, accessible by ladder.
Although by this time industry and commerce were rising pursuits in Danvers,
the town was still primarily engaged in
agriculture.

The jingle of sleigh bells could be heard in the clear air as this sleigh glided smoothly down Summer Street in this 1889 Kodak snapshot. The house, surrounded by land first cultivated in the seventeenth century, is the James Putnam house at 42 Summer Street. Three very distinguished Danvers residents have been sheltered under its exceptionally wide gambrel roof. James Putnam, who grew up here, was one of the Colonies' most able jurists and the man who taught John Adams law. Colonel Timothy Pickering, who farmed these acres from 1801-1804, commanded the Salem companies at the Lexington Alarm. He also held cabinet positions in the administrations of George Washington and John Adams. And finally, Phoebe Woodman Caliga, who as a little girl was the subject of her "Uncle" John Greenleaf Whittier's poem "Red Riding-Hood," lived here. She converted the barn on the property into Putnam Lodge, a popular hostelry for many years.

Some ambitious farmers like Alvah Bradstreet of East Danvers had long milk routes. Starting in 1881, Bradstreet, the man in the white overalls, delivered milk for thirty-two years, it is said, without missing a day. Pictured here on his Beverly-Salem route, he stands between two of his wagons—the open, two-horse, Medford-style wagon and the glass-enclosed wagon made by the Low Down Wagon Company of Easthampton. The two drivers, Josh Zwicker and Ernest Doty, preferred the latter. Bradstreet dipped milk from the large galvanized can into his customers' jugs. William Bradstreet, Alvah's father, and his sons began clearing their Ryal Side land in 1857. Their house and connecting barns stretched three hundred feet in length from beginning to end.

Sources of Industrial Power

What generated power in the mills of the seventeenth and eighteenth centuries was water directed by a sluiceway or culvert over or under a water wheel. These old mills were versatile in the work they could produce. They ground, pounded, cut, rolled, and carded such materials as grain, spices, chocolate, nails, lumber, leather, and wool. Tidal mills worked full strength for six to seven hours daily.

While the weight and fall of water created power for the larger mills, two industries utilized horse power. In the brickyards horses turned the pug mills that kneaded clay. And in the leather industry, a horse powered the mill wheel grinding tanbark.

Coal was the source of steam power. With its advent around mid-nineteenth century, peat sheds and piled up blocks of peat drying in the open air were no longer part of the farm scene. At this time Calvin Putnam introduced steam power to his planing mill. In 1899, power for the huge Bernard, Friedman & Company leather factory complex on Purchase Street was provided by boilers of "300 horsepower, with engines of 350 horsepower," according to publisher Frank Moynahan.

Steam generated electricity for the town in 1889 when Danvers became the first community in the Commonwealth to produce its own power. On the evening of January 2, 1889, seventy-two arc lights illuminated Danvers' streets and reflected down on the smiling, up-turned faces of small groups clustered under each lamp. In the words of a "poet" of the day, they had longed to see the electric light "outshine the glow worm's sickly rays/ On good old Danvers' broad highways." It was an experience that convinced everyone present that everyday in every way the world was getting better and better.

One of the town's longest lived industries was the Salem (later Danvers) Iron Works on Water Street begun in 1799 by a stock company headed by inventor Nathan Read. This mill first produced nails and anchors. Later it added iron rods and sheet metal. During the War of 1812, most of the anchors for the United States frigate Essex were cast here; the entire cost of the Essex was borne by Salem merchants. Besides creating a better machine for cutting nails, one that cut and headed at the same time, Read also patented a portable steam engine and an effective paddle wheel. Robert Fulton combined the last two into his Claremont, the first successful steamboat. Owned in the twentieth century by the Sylvester family, the mills ceased operations during the Great Depression.

Here is a peaceful scene that no longer exists. Even the contour of the land has changed. Following the custom that an owner lived on or next to his commercial property, Nathan Read left Salem around 1798 to oversee the construction of the Iron Works. The house that Samuel McIntire designed for him, known later as the Read-Crowninshield-Porter house, is pictured here. The fields to the right slope down to Water Street and the Iron Works. When Read moved to Maine in 1807, Benjamin Crowninshield, a former sea captain, bought the property so that he too could be near the foundry which he managed. On his death in 1837, the house had a new owner, Benjamin Porter of Marblehead, who farmed the land. About 1964 the house burned down, the hill was levelled, and a steel warehouse was constructed for the storage of cases of soda pop.

This bird's eye view is of another local industry, the Calvin Putnam Lumber Company begun in 1836. Into the second decade of the twentieth century, two- and three-masted schooners from Maine tied up at Putnam's wharves to discharge lumber for the yard and its mills. Putnam owned huge tracts of timberland in Maine and Michigan, tracts large enough to have their own villages and rail lines. In the center of the photograph is the white Harbor Street home of Ira Story. Started in 1853, his yard constructed boats for the Marblehead fishing fleet. When the fishing industry became concentrated in Gloucester, Story went out of business in 1876.

The Danversport Rubber Company on Liberty Bridge reclaimed the rubber in boots and other products. The two sections of the plant on the street were built in 1854 by Plains grocer Daniel Richards for his gristmill. The rear section was all or part of Samuel Page's earlier Danvers and Beverly Iron Works. It was Page who built the stone bridge, thus replacing the ferry that once plied between Danvers and the opposite shore, then part of Beverly but called Cape Annside by 'Port people. Nathan Read's Salem Iron Works bought out this company in 1811. Power for the rubber works was generated by five waterwheels developing 160 horsepower on a six-foot tide. The recycled rubber emerged from the factory as sheets, five feet by three feet, weighing about sixty pounds. The plant is seen here shortly before it burned down on August 6, 1897. It was rebuilt but closed soon after World War I.

This late nineteenth-century photograph
shows the Putnam sawmill on Sylvan Street.
The Putnams operated their mill for over
two hundred and fifty years, although it was
first located closer to Ash Street. Power for
this mill was created by damming up Beaver
Brook. Thus, Putnam's Pond or the mill-
pond is really a drowned meadow. The
property covered by the mill was later taken
over by the Walnut Grove Cemetery Corpor-
ation. The larger building in the background
is the Putnam icehouse.

The Ice Industry

Harvesting ice before the days of electric refrigeration took place in mid-winter and yielded locally from the mill-pond about six thousand tons of ice. Cutting and storing ice followed a series of traditional steps. First, the surface was scraped clear of snow and evened off. Next, the ice was scored about three inches deep in a grid pattern, each square being the size of the blocks to be stored.

Then, after a horse-drawn plow cut blocks to a depth of about six inches, floats or rafts consisting of a number of still-attached blocks were broken free and poled over to the shore where a conveyor belt carried individual blocks into the double-walled, heavily insulated icehouse. Once inside, each block was packed down on all sides with hay or sawdust not only to keep it from melting, but also to keep it from sticking permanently to another block.

These men, working for the Otis F. Putnam Ice Company in 1900, are standing on two narrow platforms poling ice blocks into the sluiceway under Sylvan Street. In the background a horse is seen pulling the scoring or the cutting saw. The large house on the left is the Wendell Hood house famous for its beautiful gardens of phlox, peonies, and rhododendrons. The lawns swept down to the pond.

The Otis F. Putnam ice wagon pictured here was a float in a parade. On the roof is an ice plow, and along the sides are splitting chisels, a large hand saw, and poling hooks. The smaller tools were used by the delivery-man to cut the ice blocks to the size (by weight) a housewife needed. Once an axe and ice pick had cut off the smaller block, a whisk broom was brushed over the surface of the ice to remove the shavings and chips. The iceman then seized the block with tongs and hoisted it over his shoulder. Protected against the wet and cold by a heavy rubber apron, he placed the ice in the kitchen or pantry ice box. Pictured with the float are (from left) Benjamin Sullivan, Saul Clark, Nelson Butler, and the boys—Carl H. Putnam and Philip C. Putnam.

The Shoe Industry

The earliest industries in Danvers were tanning, brick-making, pottery, and the production of nails, iron rods, and anchors. A manufacture like tanning begot a number of subsidiary industries like shipbuilding to procure hides, particularly in Africa, Asia, and South America.

The principal industry dependent on tanning, however, was shoe production. In the 1770s Zerubbabel Porter began what is reputed to be America's first shoe factory in a two-story building on Locust Street. By the 1830s shops extended along this road into Danvers Plains.

In the late 1840s Danvers (present-day Danvers and Peabody), was producing 1,150,300 pairs of boots and shoes annually. By the turn of the century, one factory alone, Clapp & Tapley, was capable of turning out 1,000 pairs a day. In addition, lasts, heels, wooden pegs, and boxes were being manufactured as separate businesses serving the shoe industry, and express lines conveyed cases of shoes to retailers.

A most ambitious "house portrait" is this wonderful photograph taken in the 1870s of the C. C. Farwell Shoe Company in Putnam Square. About 1850, Samuel W. Spaulding built this, the largest shoe factory in Danvers at the time, with the detail one would expect to find on a fine house. While the workers are dressed in heavy clothing, it was a warm day. Note the window shades used as awnings to keep out the sun and to allow more air into the factory. Clearly, it was important to the workers to be caught by the camera no matter where they were. In 1924 the town bought the property and hired Lester Couch to turn the building into the Central Fire Station.

The Martin Kelley Shoe Company in this circa 1906 photograph was started by an Irish immigrant who came to the United States in 1860. He lived with his aunt Kitty Curley on Holten Street. In 1865, he married Ann McCarthy and moved his small shoe factory from the corner of Adams and Pine Streets to the Holten Street house he had purchased from his aunt. During the economic depression following the Civil War, he temporarily suspended production. His next factory was in Tapleyville in the Agawan Red Men's building. Burned out in 1898, he immediately leased the factory next door and increased his output.

In neither the exterior nor the interior of the factory were there any frills. The office interiors where buyers would be received were the only finished areas. This picture of the office staff shows the matchboard paneling, the paneled doors, and the molded framing around doors and windows. All these surfaces were varnished. Members of the Kelley family worked in the factory. Martin Kelley's daughter Agnes was the bookkeeper; her sister Mary was in charge of the stitching room; and on their father's death in 1908, their brother Thomas took over the management. Agnes is seen here holding a ledger.

These men, with their foreman in the foreground, worked in the cutting room. The Kelley factory's specialty was "Growing Girls" shoes. After the removal to the new factory in 1898, children's and misses' shoes were added to the line. With all its windows, this factory, like others of the day, had good natural lighting in otherwise unfinished and unpainted work areas. Wiring for lighting and the machines was exposed, running along the rafters and down the studding.

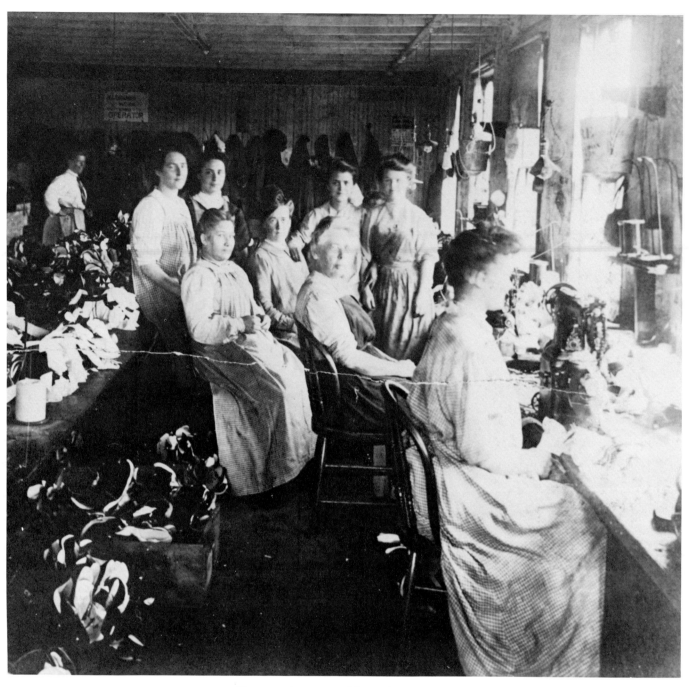

Here were the women of the stitching room. The seated, white-haired woman is Mary Kelley. There are no amenities for these women with the possible exception of the suspended lights over their benches. Note the galvanized fire buckets hung from brackets between the windows. Their effectiveness is debatable considering the number of serious fires this company experienced in a twenty-year period. Around 1917, the whole factory was, as the saying went, "sold lock, stock, and barrel" to a New York firm.

The Brick Industry

What is industrial about this placid 1880s scene on Porter's River? It's the shed roof on the left on the large drying shed of Ellen Carr's brickyard. Along the banks of Porter's River and on Endicott Street, clay beds went down twelve to fifteen feet. In one area off Liberty Street, it went down forty feet. Starting in the eighteenth century, brick-making was one of the town's largest industries. The peak decade was the 1870s when the Kirkbride Building was being constructed at the State Hospital. In the 1880s there were as many as ten yards producing five million face and common bricks annually. Mansions like the three Starbuck houses on Nantucket Island, business blocks and factories in cities like Providence, Rhode Island, even federal fortresses along the Atlantic coast were all constructed of Danvers bricks. What brought an end to the trade was the heavier use of cheaper cement blocks. Elliott Street is in the foreground.

The Local Business Scene

While prosperity and a large building boom were not without setbacks in the years 1880-1910, particularly in the Panic of 1893, the town and its commercial enterprises did very well. Although each village had its own business center, Danvers Square, the commercial and municipal heart of the town, expanded and changed dramatically. New commercial buildings replaced the large Greek Revival shop-and-home structures.

A good part of this success one local editor attributed to the fact that Danvers businessmen kept prices down to "favorable figures to the consumers." And local citizens, in return, were "wise enough to patronize the home merchants."

Actually, the Square was the shopping center for many of the surrounding smaller towns. Grocers maintained several wagons and advertised they made home deliveries for a radius of fifteen miles. Housed in the upper stories of most of the buildings were community halls, social clubs, shoe factories, tradesmen's workshops, and apartments.

In the early 1890s, Danvers Square had a wide and uncongested thoroughfare. Maple Street was widened as a result of the great fire of June 10, 1845, when the blaze leaped across the street burning down buildings on both sides. In the days of unpaved roads, the dust in summer was kept down by horse-drawn sprinklers, often followed closely by a group of barefoot boys. In winter huge rollers were employed to pack down the snow so that sleighs could pass more easily. Spofford's store on the left was on the corner of Maple and School Streets. He sold much of the Danvers souvenir china that collectors treasure. Dr. Frederick Baldwin, later the first chief of staff of Hunt Memorial Hospital, lived in the house on the right.

Maple Street, a few decades after the preceding photograph was taken, illustrates the growing, evolving nature of the business center. The hitching posts in front of the 1897 Colonial Block on the left were soon to become more ornamental than useful. Livery stables at either end of the Square would be converted into garages. Leland Ross, whose hardware store is the first shop on the left, became one of the town's first automobile dealers. The GARAGE sign on the right points to a building where Ralph O. Hood, inventor of the self-starter, worked on some of his inventions. Some of the earlier, plainer buildings lining the street have been replaced by larger, more ornate ones. The popular Old Berry Tavern in the center had broad piazzas and graceful, fan-lighted entrances. Increased traffic, a boon to merchants, ruined business for the tavern since many guests had come to enjoy the summer season in a quiet and peaceful rural community.

Perley's market stood on the corner of Maple and Conant Streets from 1800 until 1941. Charles N. Perley assumed ownership in 1886 and sold groceries, specializing in meats, dry goods, and rum. The building next to the market, also owned by Charles Perley, housed the post office. This was convenient as Mr. Perley was postmaster during Grover Cleveland's second administration and during William McKinley's presidency. He was noted to have "labored indefatigably" to establish free delivery of mail in Danvers, a reform that was instituted in 1900 under another postmaster.

The Square's fine Italianate structure, shown here in 1870, was built for the Village Bank in 1854. Reorganized as the First National Bank of Danvers in 1864, it weathered the financial highs and lows of the economy, including the crises of the Civil War and the Depression of 1893-1897, and became the Danvers National Bank in 1904. The national bank shared half the ground floor of the building with the Danvers Savings Bank. During the period this latter institution served "especially. . .the working classes, among whom it encourage[d] thrift." The Danvers Historical Society rented rooms in the bank block as well, from 1889 until 1897. On Thanksgiving Day of that year, a fire caused the organization to move. Its collection was saved from the fire and relocated to the Community Block.

Daniel Richards and his son Austin ran the
grocery and West Indies goods store at the
corner of High and Elm Streets from 1841
when Daniel built it until 1890 when Austin
sold it after his father's death. In the 1890s,
Benjamin Crombie owned the store which
shared quarters with a stove and plumbing
supply company. In front of the building is
an express wagon. Several express companies operated in the Square, including
Marston's and Pettingell and Barry's.

Grocers Beal and Abbott, who kept this store in the 1890s at 34 Maple Street, were believers in the power of newspaper advertising. Their weekly ads had such leads as "We Want You to Read This Advertisement" and "Do You Like Pickles?" George Abbott is standing behind the counter. Hanging overhead are a coal scuttle, kerosene cans, and a wicker laundry basket. Behind the sleepy store cat, note the coal stove and the chairs where the customers relaxed and exchanged jokes and thoughts on the doings around town. Behind Abbott are large tin canisters that held mocha and Java coffee and Formosa teas. The tall customer in the grey felt hat is Jacob Marston who maintained express offices in Haverhill, Danvers, Salem, Peabody, and Lynn, "the center of the shoe interests of the United States."

Luciano Zollo, proprietor of the Bay of Naples barber shop, stands at the bottom of the steps of his shop and home in 1902. The building was directly opposite the Maple Street Church; it was in the living room of this house that the church was organized on December 5, 1844. While Zollo was the first Southern Italian in Danvers, his wife Catherine (seen behind the screen door on the left) and other early Italians settling in the area came from around Genoa. Like most other ethnic groups coming to America around 1900, they assimilated quickly. Anastasia Zollo, the girl seated in the chair, and her sister Audrey became graduate nurses. Their brother Paul served as a state representative from 1953-1964. Moved back later, this structure is now at 7 Lummus Avenue.

Proud proprietor Lorenzo W. Lovelace poses before his establishment at the corner of Elm and Page Streets in this 1902 photograph. Lovelace owned store and stock valued at eight hundred dollars together with a bicycle, horse, and carriage. He was a boarder in a house on Oak Street. A contemporary advertisement of the Elm Cafe offered, "When in want of a meal or a light lunch of any kind, call at the only place in Danvers handy to electrics and steam railroad. Excellent service. Everything neat and clean." The front window includes a sign "Yes, we sell original Moxie," and few could pass by unaware that ice cream and sodas were available within.

The Holten Street area between Pine and the
railroad tracks is given the bird's-eye treatment by a photographer in 1893. The roof
in the lower righthand corner is on the Tapleyville Post Office and Lincoln Hall, the
village community center. The church is the
Methodist Episcopal Church built in 1873
on land donated by Col. Gilbert Tapley and
his son Gilbert Augustus, owners of the
local carpet factory. The greenhouse complex on the left was owned and operated by
Edward and Charles Woodman. In 1899,
publisher Frank Moynahan wrote that it
was difficult to name "any members of the
floriculture kingdom...that are not represented in the plant house." Streets in this
area laid out in the 1870s for new development were named for Congregational min-
isters: Braman, Burroughs, Clark, Fletcher,
Rice, and Wadsworth.

Transportation

With navigable rivers, an excellent highway complex, and several types of public transportation, Danvers has always enjoyed easy access to the world's markets. For about a century, boats sailed in and out of Danversport. In 1860 there were 198 arrivals here. The coastal highway system was such that by 1760 it was possible to go by stage up to Portsmouth, New Hampshire, or down to Savannah, Georgia. In 1848, the first trains made their appearance and proved cheaper and faster than ships for carrying freight.

Once Danvers enjoyed the services of two rail lines—the Eastern (Lawrence Branch) passing through Salem and Lynn to Boston, and the Western Division starting in Newburyport and passing through West Peabody, Wakefield, and Malden to Boston.

Horse-drawn street railway cars came in 1884 only to be replaced eight years later by faster electric trolleys. In 1901 the first Danvers-owned automobile rattled into town.

Photographer Frank Cousins took this panoramic view of Danversport in 1891 from the rear of the George Jacobs house. The three-masted schooner is discharging a load of coal, probably from Pennsylvania, at the Lore and Russell coalyard at the end of River Street. Across the river, East Danvers is clearly a farming district under the shade of Folly Hill. The steeple to the left of the schooner is on the Baptist Meeting House. There are two chimneys visible. The one to the right is part of Calvin Putnam's saw-mill. The one on the left is part of Woodman Brothers-Ross box factory on Mill Street. The house closest to the camera is the Stetson house located at the end of the lane beside the Riverbank estate.

Job V. and John Hanson were millers and
dealers in flour, grain, meal, and feed. During the second half of the nineteenth century
they operated a mill on the narrow bridge
over Waters River, giving their address as
"Mill at Danvers Iron Works, Mass." The
mill's accessibility to transportation is
clearly illustrated in this photograph taken
by Lefavour & Clough of Beverly in 1881.
While horses and wagons pass in front, the
two-masted schooner George P. Trigg from
New York is tied up to the rear of the building with a cargo of corn. When the mill
burned down in 1896, the Hanson's nephew,
William Penn Hussey, bore a great part of
the expense of widening the bridge and
making a small park-like area of the tri-
angular strip of land where Water and
South Liberty Streets come together.

Simple, refined, restrained—*all these adjectives describe this elegantly proportioned Federal style riverfront store seen in a circa 1870s photograph. An architectural gem, it was built prior to 1832. Jonas Warren opened a grocery business in this Water Street location in 1841. Warren, whose wharf was in the rear, was the first to import flour and grain for inland communities. He and his sons, Aaron and Harrison, next succeeded in the coal business. In the 1870s, they brought in lime and cement, often in their own ships, Jonas Warren and General Taylor, for the construction of the Kirkbride Building at the State Hospital. By the 1890s, the Warren building, stripped of its shutters, was used as a leather factory producing "India-tanned dongola kid." In the twentieth century, Samuel Kolb used the building for his junk shop. Then, sometime before 1927, it was torn down after a fire, and its bricks salvaged for re-sale.*

The old river port is in a state of slow decay a half century after the arrival of the rail-roads in 1847. The wharves in the fore-ground were owned by Maj. Moses Black, whose long, rambling house across the street was described by his granddaughter Maria as "opposite an arm of the sea down from

Beverly bridge." On the other side of the Crane River is the Lummus and Parker gristmill. The large house on the hill was 'Port merchant George B. Dennett's. The boat is a reminder that for many years Swampscott-style dories with their almost pointed sterns were built here. Around

1830, two local boatbuilders—Benjamin Kent and "Long Jim" Carr—rowed in one of their dories from St. Johns, New Bruns-wick, to Danversport in ten days. In the twentieth century, Jesse Hammond, boat-builder and carpenter, had his yard nearby at 28 Water Street.

The steam locomotive Saco, built in the
1860s or 1870s, is pictured here at the coal
pocket in the area known as Beaver Brook.
In the days of steam such fuel piles and also
water tanks were located along a rail line to
keep the engine running. With its tall smoke
stack and prominent cowcatcher, the Saco
resembles pictures of the two locomotives at
Promontory, Utah, on May 10, 1869, when
the golden spike was driven into the last tie
of America's first transcontinental railroad.
Present on that day was Danvers native
General Grenville Dodge, chief engineer of
the Union Pacific Railroad.

This train, with its combined passenger,
baggage, and mail section, has stopped at
the Plains before proceeding on to Danversport. The largest of the town's nine depots,
the Eastern Division station is shown here
on its original site on Essex Street near the
corner of Elm. In the area between the
Eastern and Western Division stations on
the Plains were freight houses and a round-
house with a turntable for changing the
direction of a steam engine.

The Western Division station off Hobart Street was the prettiest of the nine stations in Danvers. Italianate in style, its main features were the number of arched windows and decorative brackets supporting its broad eaves. The local stations in 1899 were Asylum, Collins Street, Danvers Junction (the Plains) between the Eastern and Western, Danversport, Putnamville, Tapleyville, and Ferncroft. All stations were heated, and station agents were given awards by the Boston & Maine for the neatness and attractiveness of their depots and the grounds around them.

The Danversport station was distinguished by that type of architecture called Stick style, characterized by projecting gables and exposed bracing and different types of exterior siding. The gentleman in the bowler is probably the station agent J. C. Williams. The monument to the left of the depot was dedicated to Col. Israel Hutchinson in 1896. The colonel was a veteran of three wars: the French and Indian War, the Revolution, and the War of 1812. He was also an early 'Port miller who died at age eighty-four after suffering a fall while clearing a water-wheel of ice.

On the Danvers Square of the 1880s a horse drawing a light carriage has paused at the watering trough placed where horses pulling the trolley cars could drink. The curves of the tracks, especially those leading to Salem, were so extreme that it was part of an oiler's job to grease the tracks regularly to keep down the screeching of iron wheels on iron tracks. A Danvers-Peabody horse car has stopped in front of the business block that Daniel Richards had erected in the 1840s. For some years Ernest Foss had a restaurant here where trolley passengers could find "Lunches put up to take out." On the second floor, the Windsor Club, as exclu-

sive social organization of young businessmen and professionals, had a suite of five rooms. Beyond Richards' barn, part of his

grocery business, is his circa 1842 Greek Revival home.

This circa 1890 street railway horse car was one used during the summer. It has its canvas sides rolled up here, but in case of rain, the conductor would let them down quickly. The first horse-drawn cars came to Danvers in 1884 from Salem. In 1892 they were superseded by electric trolley cars, called "Electrics" by the passengers. Both types ran from one end of town to the other, opening up previously remote areas to building and development. Note this old horse car's advertising panels. The panel for Lydia Pinkham's nostrum for female complaints caused males of the day to create a number of spurious claims for the company such as "A baby in every bottle." The old gentleman in the front seat was identified on the back of the photograph as Dr. Warren Porter, who was a Civil War naval commander.

An old glass-plate negative shows an electric or trolley car running down High Street. The picture was taken from the porch roof of the Old Berry Tavern. The house on the left, now at 21 Park Street, was willed to Mehitabel (Berry) Sperry in 1873. Harvey Pillsbury's large wooden block on the right at 10 High Street dominated the lower end of the Square. On the third floor Pillsbury manufactured light carriages, top buggies, and sleighs. The second floor had a commodious hall, "nicely furnished with stage and scenery, piano, opera chairs, and settees," accommodating an audience of four hundred. The building was razed in 1937. In 1906 George Curtis had the house on the corner moved back to 20 Park Street. Curtis then built a livery stable that he converted into the Red Arrow Garage in 1913. The house just past the next corner was owned by banker William Weston. Also visible is the old Park Street School.

In the 1890s the car barns on High Street were the property of the Lynn & Boston Railway Company. These barns which housed horses between their tours of duty were later joined by a connecting wing, and bays were installed as garages for trolley cars. Traditionally the barns were the boundary between the Plains and the 'Port. When they became the property of the Massachusetts Street Railway Company, their use was discontinued, and they were vacant for several months. At 1:15 a.m., the morning after the 'Port won its first Twilight League Championship, in 1927, the barns were burned to the ground, it was claimed but never proved, as a continuation of the 'Port's festivities.

As traffic increased on the main routes, it became more difficult to keep roads clear after a snowfall. Here some farmer's heavy pung has cleared a sidewalk for pedestrians; but before the town's large, horse-drawn rollers have had a chance to pack down the snow, sleighs have already broken a passageway on the street. The photographer for this winter scene stood about where Milton Road joins High Street. The church on the left is St. Mary of the Annunciation Church, and the house beyond it was 'Port storekeeper Jonas Warren's house, later Kerans' Funeral Parlor. All of this scene changed in the first decade of the twentieth century when a Swedish-American contractor, Hans Svenson, put in a dead-end road called Hamilton Street opposite the church. Then in 1937-1938 the area changed again when Route 128 went through wiping out everything seen here and Hamilton Street.

Bicycling was a popular and healthful pastime at the turn of the century. It was so widespread that communities were forced to keep their roads smooth for it, thus providing a suitable surface for the automobile when it came along. Mabel Spofford and her brother Ralph show off new bicycles by the shed of their home at 8 Cherry Street. Newspaper advertisements at the time featured the Keating bicycle with double roller chain and the Eclipse with "automatic coaster and brake." Safety features on the Spofford bicycles included bells and tool kits.

Only a single arc light illuminated the inter-section of Locust and Poplar Streets in 1893. But that electric light was far superior to anything previously used for street lighting. For a history of the Electric Light Depart-ment, Thurl Brown identified the town's last lamplighter as Austin L. Gould. In 1889 Gould became the town's first electric line-man. Tall elms tower over unpaved roads in the photograph. The trolley tracks were later pulled up in World War II for scrap metal. The mansion on the right, 28 Poplar Street, was built about 1856 by shoe manufacturer Charles Henry Gould. The circa 1845 Putnam-Emerson House on the opposite corner was built by lumber dealer Calvin Putnam.

A rich man's toy in 1901 when this photograph was taken, the Stevens-Duryea Runabout was manufactured in Springfield, Massachusetts, at the Stevens Arms and Tool Company by J. Frank Duryea. In 1905, Duryea won the first automobile race held in the United States in a similar car. The single driving lever or tiller of this gas buggy controlled steering, acceleration, and gear selection. The vehicle could travel at a speed of twenty miles per hour and sold for around fifteen hundred dollars. The driver here is Dr. Edward H. Niles, whose practice as well as his home was at 66 Elm Street. His passenger is the co-owner of the automobile, Edgar J. Powers.

"Uncle Walter, Aug. 5, 1896" by unknown photographer.

❧ THEIR FACES ❧

At the turn of the century, as the economy grew and the population changed, society began to adjust its visions and expectations of itself. The nature of work and jobs was altered, and with it the way men, women, and children viewed themselves and each other. The time from the Centennial until just after the First World War was a period of substantial redefinition of the roles of husband, wife, mother, father, man, woman, and child.

When the economy was almost wholly agricultural, men's and women's partnership in the family enterprise—the farm—was recognizable. As more and more men went to work in factories or businesses, as wages and profit became the measures of success, those left with the responsibility for household labor and the rearing of children for which they did not earn a wage—women—began to look as if they were doing something other than work. In the moral sphere, society came to believe that women must be the repositories of morality, affection, and human kindness for the nation. Thus, men and women stood economically and socially farther apart from each other at the time of the Centennial than they had at the Revolution.

Reformers at mid-century had sought sweeping social change for women aimed at gaining economic and social parity. Based on a broad vision of equality they argued against the belief in "separate spheres" that led to discrimination. By the end of the century, the battle for women's rights had been transformed, and centered almost completely on the franchise. Using and bolstering traditional assumptions about women's special purity and virtue, suffragists demanded the vote because they were different, capable of raising the morality of government. This argument ultimately succeeded. The cause for female enfranchisement was one of many reform movements of the period. Men and women worked together, as they uneasily had done in the cause of abolition, to end abuses of power, to reform social institutions, and to protect individual opportunity. One of the targets of reform was the treatment of children.

Children, like women, it was argued, were endowed with special purity and virtue. Earlier in the 1800s, parents trained children, cultivated and formed them, believing children to be capable of goodness. By century's end, childhood itself defined goodness for adults. Children provided the best examples of innocent, moral behavior, and were to be nurtured and cherished. They had special needs, before unrecognized, and a right to happiness beyond basic care and shelter. Increases in income were channelled toward children. Brightly colored, inexpensive toys and games appeared in abundance and encouraged play, a pursuit that a few generations previous might have labelled "idleness."

The makeup of the family changed. The great majority (about eighty percent) of households still consisted of the nuclear family (married couple with or without children, including no other relatives), but the number of children declined. Women ended childbearing at an earlier age than they had in previous generations for a number of complex reasons. On a farm children could contribute to the family enterprise, but in a wage-based system, one with child labor laws, children no longer were capable of enhancing family income. Infant mortality declined as diet and medical care improved; it was no longer necessary to have many children to ensure the survival of a few. The reduced size of the nuclear family meant that households in which all children were teenagers became common. By the end of the century, the concept of "adolescence" developed. Educators, psychologists, and reformers redefined youth, making adolescence an age for intellectual and spiritual development, equipping young people to cope in a changing social order.

Members of the Charles Kerans family are gathered around their dining room table at 24 Conant Street, now the site of St. Mary of the Annunciation Church. Kerans was one of the most inventive and successful of the Danversport leather manufacturers. He was the first to develop a formula to create a russet-colored product, thus breaking a monopoly held in Europe. Russet was the color favored worldwide for carriage harnesses and luggage. His children were fun-loving and popular, and entertained schoolmates at school functions in their home. Seated beneath the elaborate electric chandelier are (from left) Byrne Handy (a friend), Ruth, Paul, Plummer, Rachel, Katherine, Naomi, Thomas, Rebecca, Elizabeth (Mrs. Charles Kerans), and James.

This unusual family grouping was photographed by A. O. Elwell at his studio in 1892. Andrew Nichols, a well-known civil engineer and surveyor as well as an antiquarian and charter member of the Historical Society, stands at left. Son Andrew, the postmaster at Asylum Station, stands on the right while three-and-a-half year old grandson Andrew is seated between the two. Behind the three and in front of a photographer's backdrop hangs an oil portrait of family patriarch Dr. Andrew Nichols who died in 1853. The youngest Andrew is perched on an ancient Nichols family heirloom. This oak wainscot armchair with carved geometric design and braced legs is similar to chairs attributed to seventeenth-century Ipswich craftsman Thomas Dennis. An exceptional chair, it is now in the possession of the Danvers Historical Society.

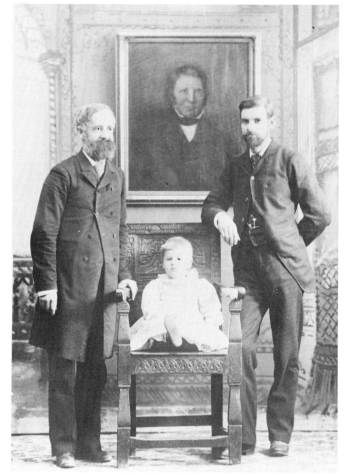

Betsy Hansen is seen in her kitchen in the house at 6 Hamilton Street she and her husband Hans, a millwright at Widen-Lord Leather Company, purchased in 1910. Because the house was large and, for them, expensive, the Hansens took in boarders. That is the reason for the two stoves. Behind the smaller stove, Mrs. Hansen displays one of her Norwegian coffee cakes. On Sunday evenings a large smorgasbord was set out in the dining room. Following dinner, family and boarders returned to the parlor for an evening of home entertainment, usually singing around the upright piano played by the Hansens' daughter Astrid.

When Miss Marcella Perry, listed as a nurse, boarded at a house on the corner of Essex and Cherry Streets, she was obviously successful at the science of midwifery. She is pictured here in the 1880s with two of her latest deliveries at a gathering of children she had brought into the world. The large wicker carriages with their lacy parasols and graceful "running gear" were handsome and expensive. An 1888 advertisement in the Danvers Mirror noted that on one make of carriage only two screws needed to be unloosened to detach the body so that it could be carried indoors to be used as a cradle. Lace-edged parasols were made of silk tamatave, satin, lace, or pongee. Wood-topped carriages could be lined with broadcloth, silk, plush, French cretonnes, silk and wool sateens, or figured silk tapestry.

Augustus P. Fowler, a local tanner, took a great interest in natural history. Posed here like the subject of a Samuel F. B. Morse portrait, he holds a brush he used for his watercolor studies of Essex County birds and their eggs. Fowler and his brother Samuel had time for scientific study and municipal service because their large business only tanned leather, a process requiring a few hired hands. A third brother, Henry, known in his youth as the King of the Cannibal Islands after he was shipwrecked in 1831 at the Fijis, was also a partner. When Augustus's wife Emily and their twins died in 1843 shortly after the birth of the babies, she was laid out in her casket with a baby under each arm. Although still a young man (he died in 1894), Fowler never remarried.

On September 3, 1888, Harriet P. Fowler, Augustus's niece, sat for her picture on the veranda of her father Samuel's house at 12 Cherry Street. A fall in youth made her an invalid. She spent her days, as much as possible, out of doors on the porch, built especially for her, studying the flowers, reading, and writing. Hattie aspired to be a poet and probably received help from her father's good friend, John Greenleaf Whittier. Her poems like "The Three Smoking Husbands," "My Sleeping Father's Lovers," and "My Balcony" are not among the period's masterpieces. However, her scrapbooks, writings, and other bequeaths to the Essex Institute remain valuable resources for scholars. In her will, she left three thousand dollars for an assistant librarian whose main duty would be the care and display of these materials.

Photographed shortly before his death in 1883, Josiah Mudge sits in a wicker chair in his front yard at 113 Centre Street. Born in 1811, this now weary but noble appearing old man was reputed as "the best carpenter of his day in Danvers." Mudge worked as a local contractor-builder for about twenty years beginning in 1838 after which he took up farming. The houses he built were typically of the two and one-half story ridge parallel to the street, or the one and one-half story cottage variety built with simple Greek Revival styling. His own house constructed in 1844 exhibits a front door flanked by glass side lights and grooved pilasters. Mudge's major work was done prior to the Civil War. During the era of the turn of the century, his building tradition was carried on by other such local craftsmen as Joseph M. Whittier, Francis A. Couch, Nathan T. Putnam, Elisha B. Peabody, and Walter L. Barker.

Harriet Page Black, the daughter of John and Mary Page, is seated in her Eastlake parlor. In 1835 she married Moses Black, Jr., and went to live in the large duplex house at 27-29 Water Street constructed by Maj. Moses Black for his sons William and Moses. Landseer etchings like the one of Highland stags on Harriet Black's wall were familiar sights in Danvers homes as they were throughout the English-speaking world. Harriet and her husband had ten children. Those children, like all of the major's other grandchildren, liked to visit him and their grandmother, Phoebe, regularly, but especially on New Year's when they received the nickels saved up all year for them by their grandparents.

Shoe manufacturer George B. Martin is seen here at Elmhurst with one of his race horses. Martin owned, trained, and raced Danvers Boy, the fastest stallion in the world at the time. When Danvers Boy was sold in 1869, Martin received twenty-five thousand dollars. Elmhurst and its grounds at 145 Holten Street was Martin's estate. In the nineteenth century wealthy men took great pride in their horses. The Danvers Riding Park behind the former Holten High School on Conant Street was laid out in 1873. Martin and other shoe manufacturers like O. N. Fernald raced their pacers and trotters here. In 1913 the Danvers Improvement Society bought the property, landscaped it, and then presented it to the town for a park.

Standing almost opposite the corner of
Locust Street and Butler Avenue are two
attractive young women, Gladys and
Caroline Damon, the daughters of
Henrietta and Frank C. Damon. Their
father wrote an amazing number of historical articles for the Salem Evening
News on Essex County communities, especially Danvers and Marblehead. Gladys,
who graduated from secondary school in
1908 four years ahead of her younger sister,
earned her bachelor's degree from Boston
University, and then returned to Holten
High School, where she became a much
beloved teacher of business subjects.
Caroline married Cyrus F. Newbegin, the
owner of the local news agency. For many
years Newbegin wrote the "Danvers
Doings" column in the news.

Between 1880 and 1910, violent crimes, often the result of intemperance, demonstrated that the Women's Christian Temperance Union had more to worry about than whether or not dancing was morally beneficial. (Their conclusion was that it was not.) In 1910, a drunken landlord, in the act of striking a boarder, was shot dead by the frightened man. In another incident, Albert Learoyd, pictured here, and four members of his household were almost killed when their breakfast tea was laced with arsenic on the morning of November 7, 1896. The twist in this attempted murder was that it was the victim, often drinking to excess with some of his farmhands, who was nearly dispatched by a sober hand, a romantic bachelor, in the belief that Learoyd was abusing his attractive young wife. Later, a changed man, Learoyd became interested in civic affairs and served the town as selectman in the 1920s.

Glimpses into a Family Album
Herbie's Life down on the Farm

A glance at the Richardson-Trask group picture suggests an industrious, but mirthless, farm family. As demanding as farm work was, these three generations of Danvers farmers found time for relaxation and fun. A number of sometimes overexposed candid photographs from an old album show the family picnicking on Horse Pasture Point, where they owned a meadow, and Charles Trask proudly showing off his sturdy plow horses and his stout hogs. The best of the pictures were taken of Herbie Trask with his pets.

Herbie was born George Herbert Trask on July 24, 1890, the son of Charles and Esther (Richardson) Trask, who were married in 1872. Besides Herbie, they had an older son and two daughters. Clearly, however, Herbie was the family's favorite.

He attended the Liberty Street Elementary school, practically in his backyard, and the 'Port School. But Herbie's was a short, happy life. On July 18, 1905, aged fourteen years, eleven months, he died of "intestinal disease," probably peritonitis, the result of a burst appendix.*

* This family is not related to co-author Richard Trask.

George Herbert Trask, December, 1894, by A. O. Elwell

95

The Richardson-Trask family in 1891.
Seated are James Richardson and his wife,
Herbie's grandparents. Standing, left to
right, are Mary and Esther Trask, their
father Charles P., their brother Charles J.,
and their mother Esther (Richardson) Trask
holding the infant Herbie.

The homestead on Liberty Street near
Conant. Originally a one-story house, a
second floor was added to accommodate
Charles Trask's growing family.

The large 1891 barn and some of the outbuildings across the street from the farmhouse.

The Family Photographer

The following is a sampling of photographs of Danvers people taken around the turn of the century by family amateur photographers on glass-plate negatives. These prints were selected from a large group of hitherto unpublished plates acquired over the years by the Danvers Historical Society and the Danvers Archival Center. These intimate peeks into middle-class Danvers homes reveal much more of the flavor of the period than staged professional photographs often show. Unfortunately, most of the people's identities are now lost to us, but their existence as real people cannot be denied thanks to the marvel of the camera.

"Mr. Nicholson and Whitney, 1897."

"Sewing-room scene, May 1, 1897."

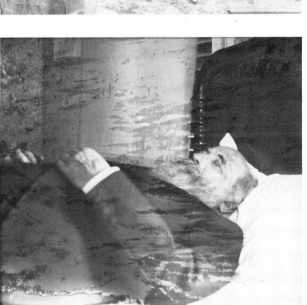

Henry White, dead from Bright's Disease, 1897.

The James O. Perry family.

Danvers Town Hall and High School, 1902.

❧ THEIR INSTITUTIONS ❧

As social and family roles changed at the turn of the century, public institutions assumed a growing presence in everyday life, taking on responsibilities formerly performed in other ways, or perhaps not required at all. New concerns for the social order pressured by a growing population, for the special needs of children, and for the betterment of everyday life, brought about changes. Familiar institutions were expanded or new organizations created to meet the growing needs of townspeople.

The town provided more services at the end of the century than it ever had before, creating an orderly environment, and making innovations commonplace. Danvers was the first town in Massachusetts to establish municipal lighting when in 1888 it appropriated $15,000.00 to build an electric light plant. The fire department employed an electric alarm system in 1895. Technology had not yet affected the police force, which in 1899 consisted of five constables and a chief of police; the department cost the town $2,718.27 that year. The street department worked on making concrete sidewalks and macadamized roads. In 1894, Danvers hired a forester to take care of "the wonderful trees on its streets."

Where municipal government left off in the improvement of daily life, other organizations picked up. The Peabody Institute trustees maintained the library for the cultural betterment of its residents. The Danvers Improvement Society, organized in 1886, worked for the improvement and ornamentation of the roads, sidewalks, and grounds of the town, observed Arbor Day yearly by planting trees, and raised money for the purchase of public parks. The Danvers Women's Association, a philanthropic and educational organization founded in 1882, supported a kindergarten, sponsored high school essay contests, and paid for prominent lecturers to enlighten the town. The longstanding cause of temperance was taken up anew in 1871 when the Catholic Total Abstinence Society formed. The Danvers Historical Society was organized in 1889 to promote historical, literary, and scientific study. These associations worked for the betterment of the intellectual and spiritual life of the town. Still a strong presence were the institutions that had traditionally assumed these responsibilities—the churches. Mirror Press's 1899 *Danvers, Massachusetts* carried its descriptions of the town's economic advantages even to its spiritual life: "[The churches] are of a decided economic value to the community because of the spirit of unity and fraternity which they develop." There were ten churches in town: First Church (formed in 1672), Baptist (1781), Universalist (1815), Maple Street Congregational (1844), Annunciation (1854), Calvary Episcopal (1857), Unitarian (1865), Methodist (1871), Seventh Day Adventist (1877), and Church of God (1899).

The American impulse for reform sparked interest in the long Cuban war for independence from Spain. Among many motivations for intervention in the war was a concern for halting the bloodletting and for exporting American reformism. The Danvers Light Infantry, Company K, entered the service of the U.S. Army when the call went out for volunteers in the Spanish-American War.

Attention to children's needs and rights fueled changes in the education system. The kindergarten movement took hold in Danvers, advocated by one of its strongest proponents, Anne L. Page. New and imposing school buildings appeared—Maple Street, Tapley, Wadsworth, and Danversport. The town set up a textbook supply system, furnishing to all what students had previously purchased themselves. New laws required proper ventilation in school buildings. In 1894 the town hired a superintendent of schools. In 1895 Holten High School, housed in Town Hall, was remodelled. A children's room was incorporated into the library in 1896. As the new century turned, public and private institutions assumed new responsibilities for the daily ordering of life in Danvers.

The Maple Street Congregational Church was established as the Third Orthodox Congregational Church in Danvers in 1844. On January 22, 1845, the original Maple Street church building was dedicated. On July 10, 1850, two young arsonists burned that church down. The edifice in this photograph was then constructed. At the end of the wooden fence on the left were the stables; on the right was the handsome little Western Division railroad station. In 1944 when the congregation was making preparations to celebrate its centennial, this church burned to the ground.

The women of the Maple Street Congregational Church have set up the tables in Granite Hall, the vestry of the church, for a special dinner early in this century. While there are a great variety of centerpieces on the tables, the small evergreens and the menorah would indicate the time is around Christmas. Since the present church is the third on the same site, the women of this church have had much need of such fundraising activities. On March 15, 1893, another group of women than those pictured here put on a Butterfly Supper. As The Danvers Mirror alliteratively described it, "Beautifully bedecked by bewildering butterflies, bewitchingly bathed in brightness...(it was) a brief but brilliant entertainment." Additional functions for Granite Hall have been Sunday school classes, debates, lectures, and plays, the last performed by members of Christian Endeavor.

This view of the First Church Congregational, was taken by Danvers photographer E. C. Tibbetts about 1888 just prior to a major remodelling. The congregation was established in 1672 as the "First Church of Christ of Salem Village," and this 1839 Greek Revival structure was the fourth built by the church. The interior exhibits pews and side galleries original to the structure, the pews having been numbered and sold to members for their use. An original high enclosed pulpit had been removed in about 1864 and replaced by the low podium with horsehair cushion bible rest, behind which is located a "swan's neck" sofa. The walls had been "frescoed" in about 1870. Following the extensive 1888 remodelling, at which time the galleries were removed and pews redesigned, in January of 1890 a mysterious fire destroyed all these efforts by levelling the building within an hour. By 1891 a new church had been built on the site in the Shingle architectural style. In 1978, the 1891 structure was similarly destroyed as a result of a fire.

St. Mary of the Annunciation Church on High Street was constructed in 1832 by the Universalist Society as its meetinghouse. Purchased in 1858 for a Roman Catholic church, the Gothic-style building was remodelled, enlarged, and rededicated in 1871. The first pastor was Reverend Charles Rainoni, but the pastor who had the greatest impact on the parish in its early years was Reverend Thomas E. Powers, who came to Danvers in 1885. During his pastorate, a large rectory was built, and the grounds were landscaped. Note the handsome cast-iron cresting on the roof ridge above the main entrances and the suspended arc light over the street. The church was torn down in 1937-1938 to make way for Route 128.

This high-style Gothic Revival edifice was built on High Street in 1858 for the Universalist Society. The Society had been formed in Danvers in 1815, and their new meetinghouse was designed by George Harding of Portland, Maine. The new church exhibited side buttresses, twin towers, pointed arch doors and windows, and a trefoil center window. A popular meeting place in the building was the lower level Gothic Hall where among other events one of the first demonstrations of the telephone was made in 1877. In 1925 the church was remodelled for use by Amity Lodge of Masons.

Schools

The earliest public movement to set up schools in present-day Danvers was in 1708 when Reverend Joseph Green spurred on the inhabitants of Salem Vilage to set up a schoolhouse "to teach their children to read and write and cypher and everything that is good." Grammar schools functioned in a haphazard manner throughout much of the rest of the eighteenth century until 1794 when Danvers was divided into specific districts and schoolhouses for each district began to be built. In 1816 a school committee was established to watch over the operations of these district schools.

During the late 1840s Danvers citizens reluctantly took up the subject of providing themselves with a high school, and by 1850 a high school was functioning in temporary quarters. In 1854, a new combined Town House and High School was built at the corner of Sylvan and Holten Streets, and in 1855 some sixty-seven students began attending school on the second floor. Named Holten High School in memory of Danvers' illustrious son Samuel Holten, the school later expanded to include additional class and laboratory rooms.

There were two preparatory schools in Danvers— Willard Hall School for Girls and St. John's Preparatory School. The girls' school started in a large Queen Anne style house on the corner of Elm and Page Streets. In the 1890s, it was relocated on Maple Street. When it began in 1891, St. John's prepared young men for the Xaverian Brotherhood.

An 1899 view of the Danvers Town House and High School taken by A. O. Elwell shows the building after its recent remodelling. Controversy raged in 1895 and 1896 as to whether or not a new high school at a different site should be built. A previous building expansion of the 1855 structure had taken place in 1883. The Town Meeting finally decided upon a second remodelling of the building and thirty-two thousand dollars was expended on the work.

The result was a Colonial Revival style building incorporating two new side wings with ninety-three foot high towers and support columns which flanked the earlier structure. This building continued to serve as a combined high school and town hall until 1931 when a new high school was completed on Conant Street. In 1949 the Town Hall once again was remodelled, at which time the two towers were removed.

This formal studio protrait includes the entire Holten High School teaching staff of 1899. Principal B. J. Powers earned a salary of seventeen hundred dollars a year, while the unmarried female teachers earned between five hundred and seven hundred dollars each. School studies were divided into a classical course for college preparation of four years: an English course of two or three years of useful education designed for everyday life and including such subjects as mathematics, physiology, civil government, physical geography, chemistry, physics, and French; and a business course lasting for two years. Miss Sarah Frances Richmond (seated in center) came to Holten High School in 1872 and remained there for forty-two years. She was affectionately called "Sally" behind her back. A former student would later remark of her, "I believe that no Danvers person has had more influence than Miss Richmond in instilling into the minds of our boys and girls the old-fashioned principles of New England life and good conduct." In 1927 a new junior high school on Conant Street was named in her honor.

The class portrait of the thirty-five member Holten High School Class of '93 was taken on graduation night on the steps of the porte cochere of the Peabody Institute Library. The June 28, 1893 graduation exercises were held in the Library auditorium with Mary E. Hyde (first row, second from left) giving her recitation "The Maid of Gettysburg," while Alice C. Abbott (third row, sixth from left) delivered her essay "The Choice of Companions." The salutatory oration was by Arthur C. Clark on "Development of Electricity." Mabel F. Paton (second row, fourth from left) wrote the class ode which concluded "Then let us all our efforts pledge, as now our paths divide, to help mankind and ever make the Golden Rule our guide." These graduates were emerging as adults in an America where 1 percent of the population possessed more wealth than the other 99 percent, and at a time when the World's Columbian Exposition in Chicago was demonstrating the miracles of modern science and technology. The "Panic of 1893" had begun only two days earlier and by the end of 1893 some four thousand banks and fourteen thousand commercial enterprises would fail.

These serious athletes were members of the 1896 Holten High School football team. Standing (from left) are Henry Damon, Fred Hutchinson, Ted Walker, Elmer Sillars, Tom Ryan, Lew White, Frank Legro, Percy Blanchard, and Winnie McLaughlin. Seated are Weldon Humphrey, Hiram Hook, Captain Oscar Perkins, and Bert Mains. Much about the game has been changed since this photograph was taken. The ball is smaller and the uniforms are more padded, although shin guards are no longer used. The greatest change, however, is the public's acceptance of the game. Parents once considered football too rough and the coaches too crude. Not even arguments by students that the game would end the cigarette evil and keep the boys off the streets prevailed. It wasn't until 1923 that football became a regular part of the school sports program.

A more accepted activity for high school boys than football was the Holten High School cadets. This 1893 Elwell photograph was made on the front lawn of the High School with Sylvan Street in the background. A regimen of discipline and drill was considered good experience and taught the boys coordination and good bearing. The boutonnieres that these boys from the classes of 1894-1897 are wearing seem an anomaly next to the guns, swords, and bayonets. Leading the company is Captain Elliott Perkins (in front) flanked by sword-holding Lieutenants Lewis Abbott and Charles Webber.

Miss Ada Lyford (fourth row, first from right) was responsible in 1893 for a class of fifty-three students at School District One on Park Street. She earned $390 a year. Mabel Spofford (first row, eighth from left) later recalled, "We used slates instead of paper. Most of us had double slates hinged together like a book. We had copy books for penmanship and for drawing, too. We wore long heavy underwear, long black stockings, high-buttoned shoes, and woolen dresses. My sleeves used to wear out, and I wore patched sleeves without a thought of embarrassment. Most of my dresses were made over from my mother's or Aunt Hattie Todd's. My coats and hoods were made over, too. We also wore tam-o'-shanter caps. When we were in Miss Lyford's grade six, we celebrated the first Columbus Day. It was a year late, 1893. We had exercises on the steps of the school. I read a long, lovely poem about the flag."

In an 1899 booklet on Danvers it was pointed out with pride concerning the town's education facilities, "The history of Danvers records no equivalent improvement in the same period as that of the past two or three years. Three new school buildings, accommodating one third [of the school population], have recently been built, and another is being constructed. The High School occupies its new quarters in the remodelled town house." One of the schools built during this boom period was the Tapley School on Holten Street. In 1895, $14,500 was appropriated for the school and land, and Edwin B. Balcomb designed this Colonial Revival style hipped-roof structure. The school house opened for grades 1-6 in 1897 and continued as a school until 1979 when it was readapted for use as elderly housing. This photograph was taken in 1902 when the building was decked out for the Danvers 150th anniversary celebration. At least two old nineteenth-century one-room school houses continued to function in districts of town into the second half of the twentieth century.

These two large Second Empire buildings
and their connecting wing and ell on Maple
Street were the Willard Hall School for Girls,
a boarding school preparing some of its young
women for Wellesley, Smith, and other
colleges. There were forty-two rooms here for
the various educational and residential
needs of the students who could take ad-
vance courses in languages and music. The
school was begun in 1879 by Mrs. S. D.
Merrill, a former teacher of natural sciences
at Bradford Academy in Haverhill. She
had taught previous to that at the Perkins
Institute, working there with Dr. Samuel G.
Howe, the founder. Mrs. Merrill spent several years in Britain giving instruction in
American methods of teaching the blind.
She gave one demonstration at Windsor
Castle for Queen Victoria.

This elegantly turned out group from Willard Hall School for Girls posed for the camera of the art photographer A. O. Elwell circa 1886. Although tennis rackets are displayed, the beautifully tailored dresses would not be seen on the courts—with the possible exception of the young lady seated on the right in the first row with her jockey cap, plaid skirt, and the looser sleeves of her blouse. Alumnae of Willard Hall were intensely loyal to their alma mater, attending annual summer reunions and sending out a newsletter, Willard Echoes, that kept classmates up-to-date on their careers and families.

In 1872, millionaire wool dealer Jacob E. Spring acquired a 150-acre farm in Danvers and hired architect G. M. Harding to design a residence for the site. Construction of the Victorian Gothic style mansion began in 1879 and was completed in 1881 at a cost of seventy-five thousand dollars. It was called Porphyry Hall referring to the color and texture of its stonework. Falling on hard times, Spring occupied the estate for only eleven years. It was acquired in 1891 by the Xaverian Brothers of the Roman Catholic Church to prepare young men for that teaching order. By 1907 the school had become a preparatory school taught by Xaverian Brothers. In 1912 the school purchased the Maplebank estate across Spring Street as an infirmary for students and a residence for the nuns who worked at the school.

Danvers Insane Hospital

The 240-foot-high glacially created drumlin known historically as Hathorne Hill and comprising some two hundred acres of land was purchased by the state in 1873 as a site for a hospital for the insane. Between 1874 and 1877, a massive and imposing complex was built on the idyllic location at the crest of the hill at a cost of some $1,465,000, and opened in the spring of 1878. This and similar facilities elsewhere in the state were designed "for the care of patients, rather than an asylum for the chronic insane." While plagued by cost overruns and referred to sarcastically by many as "the palace upon the hill," by 1899, the hospital employed 125 people, was partially self-sufficient, and had treated nearly 9,500 patients.

This view of the west wing of the State Hospital for the Insane was published in 1893. The design concept for the complex was known as the Kirkbride plan, whereby a large central administrative building was flanked by three separate step wings containing space for convalescent and less problematic patients, with an additional wing bisecting the line of the other wings to be used for "excited patients." Nathaniel J. Bradlee was the architect of this Victorian Gothic edifice which featured Danvers bricks, and a polychromatic stone-dressed exterior which highlighted arches, windows, and geometric patterns.

The grounds of the hospital were carefully landscaped, including the intricately designed flower garden laid out by Italian immigrant gardeners. The massive architecture of the buildings, the beautiful grounds, and the superb view of the countryside as well as curiosity about the hospital contributed to making the grounds a popular site for visitors. At times, particularly on Sundays, over four hundred visitors were not unusual. Described as "pleasure and sight seekers" by hospital administrators, one 1888 report noted that visitors "were presented with a printed request to keep aloof from the hospital buildings and refrain from conversations with the patients, as wards visited are kept in a state of considerable excitement."

The hospital gave the justifiable impression of a town-within-a-town including patients working in the bakery, laundry, boiler house, and sewing rooms. One aspect of the operation was the farm where staff and patients cultivated crops and kept cattle. In this 1880s photograph, an area below the crest of the hill just southerly of Maple Street is being cleared of rocks and boulders. Two men with a team of horses blurred by their activity stand near a low-slung rock sledge on wheels while hand tools, including a crow bar in the foreground, give the im-pression of the tediousness of removing stones. In the background a grove of ever-green trees abut the massive wooden barn and the adjacent brick Farm Hall. In an 1880 report it was noted that thirteen acres of land were plowed and sown to grass; additional land was cleared of stumps, brush, and rocks; and the farm produced, among other items, over 10,000 pounds of pork, 400 bushels of dandelions, 240 bush-els of onions, 1,800 gallons of cider, 46 tons of English hay, 8,000 pounds of squash, and 184 dozen eggs.

In 1856 American banker, philanthropist, and South Danvers native George Peabody gave ten thousand dollars for the establishment of a North Danvers branch of the Peabody Institute Library of South Danvers. Originally housed in Town Hall, the branch library was given an additional forty thousand dollars by Peabody in 1866 separating it into its own independent library with a governing Board of Trustees and allowing for a building of its own. The resulting structure was built on a four-and-one-half-acre plot of land on Sylvan Street purchased by the town and known as Peabody Park. The Gothic style library was constructed in 1869 with the purpose, in the founder's language, of "the promotion of knowledge and morality in the Town of Danvers." This view looking northerly up the aptly named "Sylvan" Street shows part of the millpond embankment on the far left, Pond Street, and the formidable building. In July 1890, a spectacular fire gutted the library, although through volunteer efforts the eleven thousand volume collection and most of the furnishings were saved.

The auditorium-lyceum of the 1869 library was located on the second floor and decorated in the Gothic manner including prominent posts and arches. The room contained seating for nine hundred people and was the scene of numerous gatherings and meetings. In this June 1890 photograph, the stage is set up for the graduation exercises of the Holten High School. Photographs of the graduates are displayed in the mounted frame to the right of the garland-bedecked stage. George

Peabody had suggested that sectarian theology and political discussions be forever excluded from the walls of the institution, and his wishes were attempted to be met. Each year the Lyceum Committee put together a series of public lectures for the edification, enjoyment, and education of the townspeople, and speakers included such notables as reformer Lucy Stone, publisher James T. Fields, and Ralph Waldo Emerson.

Following the devastating fire of 1890, the library trustees, confirming George Peabody's often quoted sentiment, "Education-a debt due from the present to future generations," voted to appropriate money for a new library building. Local resident Lester S. Couch of the Boston firm of Little, Brown and Moore designed the Colonial Revival building which was constructed at a cost of $34,200 and dedicated in October 1892. Possessing a low truncated hipped roof with a surrounding balustrade, the striking structure also exhibited much ornamental work including Palladian windows with fanlight and tracery, arched windows with swags, and two porticos with Ionic support columns. This winter view of the library is from a cyanotype print in brilliant blue used by many amateur photographers. Note the intricate arrow-topped cast iron fence which had been installed in 1869 around the original library building.

The 1893 library delivery hall shows the double delivery windows through which a librarian would deliver closed stack area books requested by a patron. The room is lighted with numerous gas fixtures since the building was open twice a week during evening hours. A cylindrical metal radiator is in the center of the room and on the other side of the folding double doors is the reading room. In 1892 the library instituted the Dewey decimal system for identifying books, and during the next year some 20,000 circulations were made of the 16,000 book library, while 450 new volumes were added to the collection. In an 1895 report, the librarian, while encouraging children's use of the reading room noted, "Many of the youngest readers handle the books carelessly and with badly soiled hands. For this reason it had been found necessary to remove most of the illustrated books." In 1896 a separate children's room was established.

The new auditorium located on the second floor of the 1892 library building contained seats for eleven hundred persons on a sloping floor making it the largest, and acoustically the finest in town. The ornate stage included a proscenium of classical style wood and plaster work including pilasters with Ionic caps. A new five hundred dollar piano, drop curtain, and scenery drops made this space very desirable for all manner of social and dramatic gatherings.

Fire Department

"From the bucket and axe brigade of the settlers of earlier years to the horse-drawn wagons and aerial trucks of the present day is indeed an evolution." So wrote an observer concerning the state of the Danvers fire department in 1899. From about 1800 to the end of the Civil War the local fire department consisted of a few hand pumpers located throughout town with companies made up of a large number of volunteers. It was a cumbersome arrangement, only as efficient as the nearness and quantity of the water source and the spirit and number of the volunteers who appeared to work the brakes. The town purchased a steam fire engine in 1874. In 1876 a town water works was established, and water under pressure was available from hydrants for firefighting, so that in 1877 the steam engine was sold, all the old engines were retired, and the department needed to utilize only hose companies. With this change in equipment, the department was streamlined to consist of one chief, four assistants, and a little over eighty call men. By 1900 there were 229 fire hydrants in town and the department included five wagons, four reels, one hook and ladder truck, three pungs, and seven Babcock extinguishers. In 1895 the town purchased an electric fire alarm system that in 1900 included thirty alarm boxes and a couple of steam whistles connected to the department. The central fire and police station was located on School Street where Hose Nos. One and Four were stationed, while various other pieces of equipment were housed in stations scattered throughout town.

The ten-man company of the Major Chase Hose No. 4 pose by their fire reel in this circa 1885 photograph. Each company included a foreman, first assistant, clerk, steward, and pipemen. Pictured here are two pairs of pipemen holding the brass pipe (nozzle) and wearing rubber coats, while other men hold various tools of the trade including an axe, gate, spanner wrench, and pry bar. The reel itself held coiled hose, a tool box, and kerosene lantern. On the alarm of a fire the reel would be pulled by the company to the fire by means of drag ropes. Attached to the metal framework of the reel just below the company name plate is a bell which would clang in warning as the reel was pulled to the fire.

In 1892 the town purchased a hook and ladder truck at a cost of fourteen hundred dollars. A contemporary newspaper reported, "The frame is of the best channel steel, thoroughly trussed and braced. On the side footboards are two sockets arranged to carry two six-gallon Babcock extinguishers. A large, roomy basket of wire runs from the rear axle for extra tools of all kinds. The wire basket for coats and hats extends from the rear of the driver's seat." This "great addition to our fire service" carried eight ladders from ten to forty-five feet long, and two roof ladders, all constructed of Oregon pine. There were also axes, bars, shovels, rakes, hooks, and chain. The hook and ladder house on Maple Street was renovated for the new truck and, "A pair of spare horses owned by Jacob Marston will be always available for the truck," from a stable across the street. This circa 1905 photograph exhibits the full company in dress uniform including driver Ben Chase and foreman Herbert C. Ham (second from right).

Members of the General Scott Hose Company No. 2 pose in front of their fire house next to 59 Holten Street in this circa 1902 photograph. Elden Swindell holds the reins to the two-horse hitch and is seated in a pung which holds hose, an extinguisher, and hard leather helmets. In winter when roads could be blocked or packed down by snow, the wheeled hose reels had difficulty getting through. Thus the pung, a sleigh with a box-shaped body and metal runners, would be used to better navigate winter roads.

This "snapshot" photograph was taken from the backyard of a house on High Street looking east towards Liberty Street on July 8, 1905. The photographer's interest is not in the unkempt grounds, the various styles of inexpensive fencing, chicken coops, and other outbuildings seldom included in photographs, but rather the billowing black smoke in the background. The Kerans leather manufacturing plant caught fire at about 1:00 p.m., and although two alarms were pulled, the electric alarm system failed, so that it took over half an hour for the fire department to arrive. Within an hour the entire complex, except for the brick chimney stack, was levelled and the fire fighters had to make great efforts to save other area businesses. The loss was one hundred thousand dollars, the largest individual fire loss to that time.

Police Chief Joseph Merrill is seated in front of his force in 1912. In this picture taken by professional photographer William Taylor, the constables (left to right) are Tom Blodgett, Michael Noonan, Timothy Connors, and Edward Price. Their duties were similar to those of a modern police force: preserving law and order. But these men went on solo foot patrols to the business and residential sections of town. They dispensed justice occasionally by a firm, swift kick. In 1880 their biggest problem was vagrancy when 263 people, mostly men, were lodged and fed in the tramp house overnight and then "allowed to go their way." When a Tramp Law was passed in May of that year permitting the force to send vagrants to the workhorse or jail, the number dwindled to eighteen through December. Drunkenness was the greatest offence police dealt with. In 1912, the ratio between this and the second greatest offence, assault and battery, was ten to one.

Company K

In early 1891 over forty enthusiastic Danvers young men organized themselves into a militia company taking the name "Danvers Light Infantry." Soon thereafter the unit was recruited into the Eighth Regiment Massachusetts Volunteer Militia with the company designation "K" and under the captaincy of Frank C. Damon.

Needing a secure place to drill and store their equipment, the Danvers company was able to acquire and convert into an armory by August 1891, a skating rink on the corner of Maple and Hobart Streets which was later further expanded to include a bowling alley and banquet room. In late September, the Danvers unit hosted a Field Day for the entire regiment, and during the afternoon a sham battle was enacted. Because of overexuberance during the sham battle, the local press reported, "Several members of the Regiment were accidently wounded by blank cartridges and bayonet thrusts."

Company K was in the center of the military and social life of Danvers during the 1890s, but these social aspects took on a serious nature as difficulties with the government of Spain escalated in 1898. On February 15, 1898, the U.S. battleship *Maine* blew up in the harbor of Havana, Cuba, killing hundreds of sailors, and by April 21, President McKinley, urged on by the popular press and a jingoistic national undercurrent, declared war on Spain. Many saw the conflict in simplistic terms. One local writer commented, "On one side were grouped liberty and humanity, and on the other superstition and ignorance, tyrannism and treachery." The United States now had a "good little war" in which territorial spoils were an attractive prize. Fanned on by the newspapers, many patriotic and adventure-seeking American men wanted to do their bit for the flag. McKinley called for 125,000 volunteers and the Eighth Regiment was called up by the governor to become the Eighth Infantry U.S. Volunteers. In Danvers, Capt. A. Preston Chase and his officers recruited a full complement of soldiers and were ordered to report by train for active duty.

At 7:30 a.m. on May 5, 1898, Company K was given a tumultuous send off by the townspeople of Danvers. A platoon of police, the Holten High School Cadets, the Post 90 Grand Army of the Republic Civil War Veterans, as well as the citizens and school children escorted the company to the railroad station. The *Danvers Mirror* reported, "At the Square the line maneuvered prettily, and cheers and other demonstrations were heard on all sides. When the train moved out there was a moving sea of flags, the air was rent with deafening shouts, and amid cheers and tears, exultation and sadness, the brave boys of Co. K left for unknown duties and unknown places."

The Eighth Regiment was sent to Chickamauga, Georgia, along with tens of thousands of other troops to await orders for Cuba, and there they remained during the summer of 1898 at a camp where typhoid fever and other diseases took their toll due to poor drainage and a malarial atmosphere. On August 19, twenty-one year old Danvers Bugler Spencer S. Hobbs died of illness.

In late August the regiment removed to Chattanooga, Tennessee, and though not in time to participate in the war, in January 1899, the regiment landed in Matanzas, Cuba, remaining there a few months on mop-up duty. By April 1899, the regiment was transported home, and on April 11, the town of Danvers put on an enthusiastic official welcome-home celebration.

Though talk of adventure and new prizes had delighted the majority, a few questioned the nation's direction. "E.A.P." wrote anonymously in the local paper in May of 1899, "I have a horror of war, and I wish to enter my solemn protest against the horrid, fiendish, hellish business in which my country has been engaged the past year, on this side of the world, and is now prosecuting among the heathen on the other." Yet these voices were drowned out by a country on the move, and sure of its direction, and many a young man from Company K would take an active role in shaping, if not the destiny of the nation, at least the future direction of Danvers.

The officers and men of the Eighth Regiment at Dress Parade on Eben Berry's fields off Conant Street now known as "Danvers Park." Dressed in their tunics and cork helmets, and presenting with bayonets fixed, the men were taking part in the regiment's fall field day on September 29, 1891.

A snapshot photograph of the Eighth Regiment's sham battle in progress taken from the opposite bank of Porter's River is looking easterly towards Elliott and Conant Streets beyond. Soldiers, their white cork helmets just discernible, dot the hill while spectators, many on bicycles, follow the action.

Capt. Frank C. Damon (seated in center) and his award-winning rifle team sit for this 1895 formal studio portrait by A. O. Elwell. The seven young men sporting forage caps strike a military pose while rifle cases, cartridges, and cartridge boxes are strewn in the foreground amid the photographer's props.

Company K drew up in front of their armory about 7:00 a.m. May 5, 1898, in full field dress including campaign hats, leggings, blanket rolls, canteens, and mess cups. The men are about to depart for the parade to the train station. Captain Chase (right) and Lt. Henry W. French (left) grasp their swords while the men stand at attention, their rifle stocks painted with identification numbers.

Lining up on Maple Street near Hobart is the male citizen escort for Company K. Predominently in derby hats and sporting patriotic pins and ties, many of these men also carry flags. The jaunty man at right with arm on hip is thirty-three year old William B. Sullivan, an 1895 graduate of Boston University Law School whose active career in law had just recently begun. A temperance man and later president of the

Danvers Historical Society, Sullivan twenty-one years later would be called on by the town to address the welcome home program for another group of young men who would survive the First World War. In that speech, Sullivan would comment, mirroring many Americans in a then-emerging and far different era, "Independence means that we go on living our own lives without becoming embroiled in the conflicts of other nations."

*Taken from an elevated position at the Old
Berry Tavern, the parade of farewell travels
down Maple Street and turns right onto
Elm. Flags and bunting decorate the Square
which is thronged with citizens showing
support for their local boys.*

The boys from Company K were not the only Danvers men to serve in the war. Jacob C. R. Peabody, who lived with his father at The Lindens on Sylvan Street, received a commission as captain in Company A of the Eighth Regiment. While in Cuba he served as aide-de-camp to General Ludlow. In these two pictures from a Peabody family photo album are a view of the wreck of the battleship Maine and a staff mess in Havana. Peabody is the officer standing at the far end of the table.

Bicycle outing, 1896.

✤ THEIR SOCIAL TIMES ✤

In the late nineteenth century, industrialism created free time previously unknown to Americans. For a nation that had grown up with a distaste for idleness, it adapted well. Work weeks shortened, down to sixty hours for many laborers by 1890. Innovations in machinery made farmers' lives easier. By the turn of the century, domestic labor-saving devices actually began to save labor. Most of the nation had more time for activities other than work or sleep. Society created for itself ways to fill the new-found hours.

Men and women were together in socially structured activities far more often than were previous generations. Sports was the best mechanism for lowering the barriers between the male and female worlds. Ice skating, roller skating, bicycling, and croquet gave couples acceptable ways to be close in public. Taking advantage of new opportunities for social contact, Americans owned over ten million bicycles by 1900. Golf's popularity swelled as well. In 1890 America had one golf course; by 1900 it boasted over one thousand, including the one in Danvers. As women participated in these activities, their dress grew less restrictive—corsets were modified, hems raised, and petticoats shed. Made of volumes of heavy fabrics, women's bathing suits remained cumbersome, however. While both sexes went to the beach, only men swam.

Other pastimes besides sports attracted people. Circuses, dramas, and musical comedies provided amusement and escape. Fourth of July celebrations, ball games, and public park activities gave people of varying social, religious, and political traditions a common experience. Events like the 1902 celebration of Danvers' 150th anniversary were times for levelling differences among the population. Men, women, and children, rich and poor, farmer and industrialist, turned out by the tens of thousands to celebrate perhaps the only commonality among them—their community.

It was first suggested at Town Meeting in 1868 to erect a Civil War memorial. Underwood & Brook of Boston drew up plans, and a 33.25-foot-tall monument of Hallowell granite was erected in front of Town Hall, and dedicated on November 20, 1870. The inscription read, "Erected by the citizens of Danvers in memory of those who died in defense of their country during the War of the Rebellion, 1861-1865," and included the names of ninety-five dead representing about 2 percent of Danvers' 1860 population. This photograph was apparently taken during Decoration Day, 1872, looking east towards Elm, Park, and Sylvan Streets. Members of the local Grand Army of the Republic encircle the wreath-decked monument, while members of a brass band are stationed at the lower left. It took some seconds to make this photographic exposure, and its effect can be seen in the blurring of the American flags as well as in the ghost-like images of a man under the "R R Crossing" and the head of a nearby horse both of which moved during the exposure.

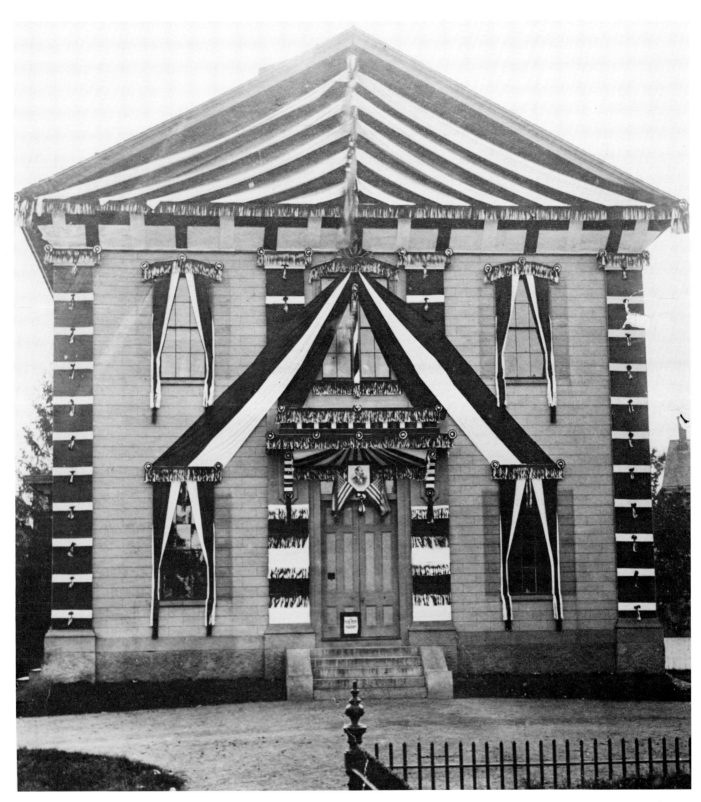

In 1854 Danvers voted to build a High School and Town House at the convergence of Sylvan and Holten Streets. At a cost of $11,148 including the land, Emerton & Foster designed and Benjamin Moore built the Greek Revival edifice described on completion as an "elegant and ornamental building." Following the death by assassination of President James A. Garfield on September 19, 1881, Danvers citizens gathered at the Town House to plan memorial services. At the request of the selectmen, B. L. Alley draped the building with mourning bunting, and on September 26, a photograph was taken of the result and sold for fifty cents a print to help defray the decorating costs. A letter to the Danvers Mirror stated, "I think the citizens of Danvers may well congratulate themselves on the elaborate and tasteful manner in which their Town Hall was draped. It surpasses anything I have seen in Boston or any Massachusetts city or town." Numerous Danvers churches and businesses were similarly draped.

On April 26, 1893, the Danvers Historical Society sponsored a meeting at Town Hall bringing together a large group of elders who had been firebrands in the anti-slavery movement from the 1830s to 1860. Society President Reverend Alfred Porter Putnam (first row, sixth from left) remarked concerning the invited guests, "You have taught us how to stand for the right, to stand for it consistently and uncompromisingly. We are all of us the better for what you have been, for what you have said, for the lives that you have lived." Among those present in this photograph made by William T. Clark are luminaries Lucy Stone (first row, eleventh from left), and Parker Pillsbury (top row at right of central gas lamp shaft). Sitting in the audience below the potted plants is local political activist Mrs. Evelyn F. Masury with her young son Alfred. This sedate group photograph belies the ferocity and extremism which others saw in these local and national reformers a generation earlier.

Nineteenth-century Danvers always celebrated Independence Day with public events, often including a parade. In this 1891 photograph taken near the corner of School and Franklin Streets, broom-holding blacksmith Dean A. Perley poses with his workmen aboard his "shop on wheels." During this and many similar parades, Perley and his men pounded out horse and ox shoes as the wagon rolled along the parade route. A bellows and vise can be glimpsed among the greenery and flags, while drover Orrin Peabody, sporting a stovepipe hat, pauses beside his yoke of oxen.

In 1892 another Independence Day parade lines up in Danvers Square. The old brick Fossa building and Hayes drug store on the corner of Elm and Maple streets are evident in the background of this professional photograph made by E. W. Merrill. A "tally-ho" loaded with fancy-clothed women and tall-hatted gentlemen was the parade entry sponsored by the ever-popular Old Berry Tavern.

The town expended seven hundred dollars on this Independence Day celebration. A scare occurred during the parade when one of the lead horses of this coach, "had a fit, and the driver was forced to turn the tally-ho with its heavy load into C. S. Richard's yard, nearly upsetting the concern." For the remainder of the parade route the coach made do with only two horses.

Danvers Square afforded many well-fre-
quented places for social exchange. The
Old Berry Tavern boasted perhaps the most
charming exterior among such gathering
spots. It stood at the corner of Conant and
High streets and is shown here as it appeared
when owned by Eben G. Berry. At the end of
the last century, Danvers was a popular
town for summer residences, and the Tavern
offered accommodations for the family who
wanted "the greatest amount of pure ozone
and the most comfortable place to eat and
sleep for the least expenditure of money."

Yet another July 4 parade winds its way
around the Old Berry Tavern and down
High Street. Spectators walk along beside
the Agawam brass band and a company of
the Eighth Massachusetts Regiment in this
mid-1890s photograph by E. W. Merrill.

What this very late nineteenth-century tableau represented is not certain. Certainly the participants saw the United States as a powerful force in the world attracting people to its shores. Although millions of immigrants were arriving annually, especially from southern and eastern Europe, few of the actors on this stage seem to be in native costume. At this time there were no English language or naturalization classes in Danvers. It wasn't until 1919 that adult alien education classes for men were first held in the foremen's lunch room of Widen-Lord Tanning Company. The following year state-approved classes were taught to both men and women.

When Louis Brown assumed ownership of the Old Berry Tavern in 1896, he set out to remodel the Greek Revival building. He removed the porches and erected new porte cocheres added to the rear wing, and put in the latest innovations—electricity, gas, steam heat, and numerous bathrooms. The whole effect, promoters claimed, was a pervasive "air of hospitality and good cheer." Renovation blended with the long tradition of the tavern to produce a public house of which Danversites were proud. This photograph of the dining rooms was published in an 1898 promotional brochure. In the mid-1920s the building was moved back, and the Danvers Savings Bank was erected on the site.

Golf was so popular at the turn of the century that the Danvers (later Homestead) Golf Club was formed in 1900 on the old Porter farm on Locust Street. Among the local families gathered here at the caddy shack are the Damons. Frank C. Damon, a newspaperman, was the leader of the project. He is seated on the lawn; his wife Henrietta and their daughter Gladys are seated to the left behind the three little girls. The course was laid out by Nicholas Brothers of Boston. Whether or not playing would be allowed on Sunday afternoons and where, if anywhere, liquor could be consumed in the clubhouse was of great concern to a few of the original stockholders. This whole area was later flooded to form the Putnamville reservoir.

Among popular small-town entertainments were mock weddings modelled after P. T. Barnum's much publicized marriage of his diminutive attraction, Tom Thumb, to Mercy Bumpus. Around 1905 Mrs. Anna Crosby of the Methodist Church in Tapley-ville provided townspeople with an especially elaborate ceremony. The wedding was con- *ducted by the "precise minister" Raymond Poor, who united in the "iron bands" of matrimony Doris Giles and Harry Eldridge. Standing up for them were Luella Eldridge and Charles S. Tapley. The bride, Doris Giles Walfield, later became the mother of four, the grandmother of twenty, and the great-grandmother of twenty-four.*

While not exactly Gibson girls, these ladies on a literary outing to the seashore favored leg-of-mutton sleeves on their jackets and shirtwaists. Miss Sarah Hunt is reading to the group. Also seated with her from left are Isadora Kenney (behind Miss Hunt), Alice Kenney, and Alice Putnam. Standing from left are Mrs. George O. Stimpson (whose parents were both murdered on a voyage to South Africa in 1892), Sarah F. Richmond perhaps on the lookout for the Hesperus, and Annie Porter. All these women were socially prominent in their day. Miss Hunt and Mrs. Kenney were both presidents of the Danvers Women's Association.

These youngsters are skating on the mill-pond around 1900. Some boys and girls from this period like Aaron Powers became proficient figure skaters. For years in the mid-twentieth century, Powers, a town employee, organized popular ice carnivals on the flooded meadow off Hobart Street. Other boys preferred hockey and arranged informal games with teams from different parts of town. East Danvers would challenge a 'Port team around 1920 to regular Saturday games on what they called New England Pond, an abandoned clay pit of the New England Press Brick Company. Each winter the saddest moment for the youngsters such as those pictured here came when the men arrived to begin harvesting the ice. Then they were sent packing to skate on much smaller ponds and frozen swamps.

Details fill this picture of a typical Danvers living room at Christmastime. On the tree are strings of popcorn, lighted candles, balls, and gifts including a doll and a football. Under it are other presents: two pairs of riding boots, a wooden shovel, a stack of plates, and an iron bank in the shape of a safe. To the right is a new sled; and to the left, a cut-velvet Eastlake chair and a footstool. The shiny new cuspidor is also a gift. It has not yet collected around it the gelatinous amber ring that Charles Dickens found so offensive in Erie Canal barge saloons in the middle of the nineteenth century. The two large formal photographs in the door and the window are also apparently gifts. This photograph was made from a glass-plate negative taken around 1900.

In many New England communities the first settlement clustered around a village common. In that part of Danvers which was the center of seventeenth-century Salem Village, a two-acre common was deeded by Deacon Nathaniel Ingersoll in his 1719 will, "to the inhabitants of Salem Village for a training place forever." The political and economic center of Danvers shifted early, leaving this area around 85 Centre Street primarily rural, though the field continued to serve as a muster ground for generations of citizen soldiers. By the 1850s the field had fallen upon rough times, and the Danvers Centre Ornamental Tree Association was formed to aid its recovery. They planted shade trees, graded the land, and erected granite boundary posts. The result of this beautification can be seen in this circa 1891 photograph. A flag pole constructed of Oregon pine and standing 125 feet high is in the center of the common. At left an early eighteenth-century house best remembered as the Upton Tavern sits adjoining the field.

By 1894 historically minded Danvers citizens wanted to commemorate the gift of the field, and on June 30, a glacial boulder, which had been shaped and inscribed, was dedicated as a monument to Deacon Ingersoll and to "The brave men who have gone hence to protect their homes and to serve their country." This E. W. Merrill photograph shows the speakers' stand located adjacent to the marker on the south tip of the training field. Among those on the platform are Abner C. Goodell and William C.

Endicott (under the umbrella). Endicott had served as Secretary of War in the Cleveland administration from 1885 to 1888, and his summer residence was just a few hundred yards away down Ingersoll Street. To the right of the front post is Judge Alden P. White seated next to Tree Association President Augustus Mudge (hat on knee). Speaking is Historical Society President Alfred P. Putnam while members of the local Grand Army of the Republic and other spectators gather around to hear the program.

Danvers Celebrates Its Birth

Like most other communities throughout the United States, Danvers yearly celebrated Decoration Day and Fourth of July with various public parades, speeches, and processions. It was in 1902, however, that Danvers far outdid any previous celebration when it commemorated the 150th anniversary of its establishment in 1752 as a separate municipality from Salem.

Among the public programs held from June 15 through June 17 were special church services, band concerts, a ball, children's entertainment, and grand fireworks at Danvers Park lasting some two hours. A Town Hall banquet brought four hundred people together to consume a catered meal featuring turkey, cold ham, tongue, lobster salad, chicken croquettes, and banana fritters followed by numerous ice creams, cakes, and long after-dinner speeches.

The most popular events of the celebration were the bonfire held at midnight on June 15 and the parade which began at 10 a.m. on the seventeenth. The *Salem Evening News* gave a backhanded compliment concerning the celebration commenting, "Somebody has said that Danvers wakes up once in fifty years. This may not be a base slander, but there is no disputing the fact that when she sets out to wake up in dead earnest there is no doubt about the result." The celebration was great fun and brought townspeople closer together, and drew thousands of others throughout the region. Its size and diversity would not be matched for another fifty years.

The spectacular bonfire stack constructed of over fifty tiers of barrels and railroad ties was set up in Danvers Park under the direction of local contractor William A. Berry. Boasted the local press, "The structure when it was done was an aspect so unique and so impressive that it might almost have seemed befitting that it should itself have stood as a monument of the occasion." Some fifteen thousand spectators watched as it was torched at midnight, June 15, sending out heat which could be felt a quarter of a mile away.

151

"The town was one blaze of color, in which 'Old Glory' predominated," as town buildings, businesses, and private residences competed with one another for the grandest display of celebration bunting. On Maple Street at the head of Conant Street, a three-span arch some eighty feet across was festooned with banners and flags and illuminated at night. On the east side but farther along Maple Street, Porter's block was draped in stars and stripes and sported a larger than life portrait of George Washington astride a white steed, while the newly built Colonial Revival William P. Radford house at 40 Conant Street showed off its grand decorations which billowed in the warm breezes of June.

Over fifteen hundred school children conveyed on forty-one floats participated in the parade. This amateur's glass-plate negative records one such float driven by "Uncle Sam" and occupied by girls representing various states of the Union.

An estimated seventy-five thousand people viewed the parade which snaked six miles throughout town and took two hours to pass a given locale. A genuine character of controversial note, William Penn Hussey, owner of the extensive Riverbank estate in Danversport, underwrote much of the parade and celebration expenses and was named the parade's Chief Marshal. Here Hussey (left) and his son Assistant Marshal J. Fred pose for a quick "snapshot." In 1916 Hussey's family erected a bronze equestrian statue across from Riverbank on Water Street featuring Hussey replete in his Chief Marshal's uniform, and looking a bit more noble in the work of art than in the flesh.

Another unit composed of children was the Peabody Cadets including in this picture an ambulance corps and a miniature horse and buggy containing several young girls representing the Red Cross. The parade has paused for a moment on Maple Street, and the stretcher bearers have put down their litters. The iron fence marks the grounds of the Maple Street School, and the long narrow building with belfry is the home for the fire department's Hook and Ladder No. 1. Over the building's front door is a heroic mural of a fireman on a ladder saving a young woman from a conflagration.

Portfolio of a Photographer's Work

E. W. Merrill in Danvers

Among the professional photographers who lived and worked in Danvers during the waning years of the nineteenth century was Elbridge Warren Merrill, born in West Newbury in 1870. Merrill's father died in early 1873, and in 1874 his mother Mary Evelyn (Pillsbury) married Leander Falls. By 1880 Merrill, his stepfather, and mother were living in Danvers in the household of his mother's brother, Harvey H. Pillsbury. The stepfather died of consumption that same year.

Little is known of Merrill's early years other than tracing his many moves in Danvers by means of the street poll lists. In 1890 he is listed as a "necktie cutter" while in 1895 his occupation is listed as "artist" and "photo-printer." It is not known just how Merrill became interested in and pursued photography, though a few prints handstamped "Photographed by E. W. Merrill, Danvers, Mass." and a group of recently uncovered glass plates reveal his discerning eye and superior technique. Merrill's work as a photographer in the Danvers area was short-lived since in 1898 he left for the Klondike and resided in Sitka, Alaska, until his death in 1929. Among other projects, Merrill photographed the Tlingit Indians over a thirty-year period.

The circa 1810 Joseph Sprague house on Endicott Street.

Maple Street near the corner of School Street.

The newly built Colonial Revival George O. Stimpson house on Elm Street, Lester Couch, architect

Probably Masonic Hall, Jordan Lodge, Peabody.

The circa 1882 Silas Conant homestead on Summer Street.

SELECTED BIBLIOGRAPHY

The authors have attempted to indicate sources within the text. In addition to town records, the *Danvers Historical Collections*, the *Danvers Mirror*, the *Salem Evening News*, and local business directories, the following were consulted:

Hanson, J. W. *History of the Town of Danvers*. Danvers: The Courier Office, 1848.

Moynahan, Frank E. *Danvers, Massachusetts*. Danvers: The Danvers Mirror, 1899.

Tapley, Harriet Silvester. *Chronicles of Danvers: Old Salem Village*. Danvers: The Danvers Historical Society, 1923.

Tapley, Charles Sutherland. *Country Estates of Danvers*. Danvers: The Mirror Press, 1960.

Zollo, Richard P. "Danvers Square: An Informal History," The *Danvers Historical Collections*, XLIII: 1967.

George W. Bell's House Being Moved, circa 1895, from Middleton to 3 Charter Street, Danvers.

INDEX

ABOUT THE AUTHORS

The authors—Richard B. Trask, Richard P. Zollo, and Joan M. Reedy—pose behind the bar in the Thomas Haines ordinary at 35 Centre Street. This "First Period" dwelling is home to Richard and Ethel Trask and their daughter Elizabeth.

Richard B. Trask is a graduate of Salem State College and Northeastern University. He is archivist for the town of Danvers. Among his town volunteer efforts have been director of the Samuel Parris archaeological site excavation; member of the Historical Commission, Bicentennial Committee, Historic District Commission; curator of the Historical Society, curator of the Rebecca Nurse Homestead; and lieutenant in the Danvers Alarm List Company. He is an acknowledged expert on the 1692 witchcraft hysteria, a past president of the Essex County Historical Association, and historical consultant for several films including *Three Sovereigns for Sarah*. A number of his articles have appeared in national publications.

Dr. Richard P. Zollo is a graduate of Bowdoin College and Boston University. He is a professor emeritus of Salem State College, where he was editor of *The English Review*. For his contribution to the life and works of John Greenleaf Whittier, he was made an honorary life member of the Whittier Society. He is also honorary historian of the Danvers Historical Society, a distinction he shares

with Richard Trask. In the field of local history, he is a past president of the Danvers Historical Society, a charter member of the Danvers Historical Commission, and a former editor of the *Danvers Historical Collections*. A frequent speaker on local history, he has also written many newspaper articles on the subject and is a writer for the *Essex Institute Historical Collections*.

Joan M. Reedy, curator for the Danvers Historical Society, was born in Youngstown, Ohio. A graduate of Youngstown State University (B.A., History, 1982) and Northeastern University (M.A., History, 1983), she received a certificate in historical agency administration from Northeastern and completed the Seminar for Historical Administration in Williamsburg, Virginia. Having worked for several historical organizations, she came to Danvers in 1984. Joan, who wrote the chapter introductions in this volume, has taught history at the University of Lowell and served as Secretary of the Bay State Historical League since 1985.